DOREEN VIRTUE

Armor of God

Biblical Help for Spiritual Warfare

First published by Amazing Grace Productions 2025

Copyright © 2025 by Doreen Virtue

All rights reserved. No part of this publication may be reproduced, stored or transmitted in any form or by any means, electronic, mechanical, photocopying, recording, scanning, or otherwise without written permission from the publisher. It is illegal to copy this book, post it to a website, or distribute it by any other means without permission.

Christian Standard Bible (CSB) Publisher: Holman Bible Publishers Copyright: © 2017 by Holman Bible Publishers Fair Use Statement: The verses in this work are used under the Fair Use copyright law.

English Standard Version (ESV) Publisher: Crossway Copyright: © 2001 by Crossway Fair Use Statement: The verses in this work are used under the Fair Use copyright law.

King James Version (KJV) Publisher: Various publishers (original 1611 edition is public domain, but modern editions are published by different houses like Thomas Nelson or Cambridge University Press) Copyright: Public domain for the original 1611 edition, but modern editions may have specific copyright for certain elements (e.g., introduction, commentary) Fair Use Statement: The verses in this work are used under the Fair Use copyright law.

New American Standard Bible (NASB) Publisher: The Lockman Foundation Copyright: © 1995 by The Lockman Foundation Fair Use Statement: The verses in this work are used under the Fair Use copyright law.

New International Version (NIV) Publisher: Zondervan (a division of HarperCollins) Copyright: © 2011 by Biblica, Inc.™ Fair Use Statement: The verses in this work are used under the Fair Use copyright law.

New King James Version (NKJV) Publisher: Thomas Nelson Copyright: © 1987 by Thomas Nelson Fair Use Statement: The verses in this work are used under the Fair Use copyright law.

First edition

This book was professionally typeset on Reedsy.
Find out more at reedsy.com

Contents

Also by Doreen Virtue:	1
Introduction	3
Chapter 1: The Armor We Need	6
Chapter 2: The Indwelling Holy Spirit	10
Chapter 3: Trusting Jesus to Fight the Battle	14
Chapter 4: Resisting the Devil	18
Chapter 5: Firm in Your Faith	21
Chapter 6: Take Every Thought Captive	24
Chapter 7: The Shield of Faith	27
Chapter 8: The Helmet of Salvation	31
Chapter 9: The Breastplate of Righteousness	34
Chapter 10: The Belt of Truth	37
Chapter 11: The Sword of the Spirit	40
Chapter 12: The Shoes of the Gospel of Peace	43
Chapter 13: Unresolved Anger and Spiritual Warfare	46
Chapter 14: Jesus' Victory and Spiritual Warfare	49
Chapter 15: Sin's Role in Spiritual Warfare	53
Chapter 16: Bad Decisions and Spiritual Warfare	57
Chapter 17: The Truth about Deliverance Ministries	61
Chapter 18: Items in Your Home and Spiritual Warfare	67
Chapter 19: Prayer and Spiritual Warfare	70
Chapter 20: When God Tests Us	75
Chapter 21: God's Pruning Process and Spiritual Warfare	80
Chapter 22: When God Disciplines Us	83
Chapter 23: Understanding Demons' Limited Power	86

Chapter 24: Don't Let the Devil Steal Your Joy or Peace	90
Chapter 25: Unequally Yoked and Spiritual Warfare	95
Chapter 26: Guilt, Shame, and Spiritual Warfare	100
Chapter 27: Reducing Your Vulnerability to Spiritual Warfare	105
Chapter 28: Insomnia, Nightmares, Sleep Paralysis and...	109
Chapter 29: Stick to What the Bible Says	113
Chapter 30: Listening to the Audio Bible	116
Afterword	119
About the Author	120

Also by Doreen Virtue:

Comfort in Christ Devotional & Coloring Book
Psalm 32 Devotional & Coloring Book
How to Avoid New Age & New Thought Deception

Note: Doreen Virtue was saved out of new age in 2017. Prior to her salvation, she unknowingly wrote unbiblical books and card products. She no longer sells this old material, but some people sell it despite her requests to not sell it. If you own any products from Doreen that were published in 2017 or earlier, please dispose of the items.

Introduction

God saved my soul in 2017 after I'd spent 33 years as a member of New Thought churches and a subsequent 26 years in New Age deception. During those 59 years prior to my salvation, I thought that I was receiving messages from God's angels. But after I was saved, those "angels" started harassing me with insomnia, because they were demons who had masqueraded as angels throughout my pre-salvation life. I had unknowingly been their spokesperson (2 Corinthians 11:14-15).

The days following my salvation were my first conscious awareness of spiritual warfare. I could sense evil presences near me, which made me anxious and unable to sleep. So, I researched how to stop spiritual warfare and found deliverance ministries and books that guaranteed they'd cast away the demons.

In the new age prior to my salvation, I'd been involved with processes similar to deliverance ministries. The new age versions were called "depossesion" and "spirit releasement therapy." I wrote and taught about these concepts in the new age. Even though in the new age, there was no belief in the devil, demons, or evil, there was a strong belief in "spiritual blocks." We believed that any problems we had stemmed from our own negative thinking, or from "negative energy" from living or deceased people. In the new age, we called upon Archangel Michael (a new age version and not the biblical Archangel Michael) to release people from negative energy or entities. We also tried to cast out these energies and entities with our affirmations and theatrical hand gestures.

So, when I came across deliverance ministries in the throes of my spiritual warfare in 2017, it seemed familiar. Deliverance ministry was based upon similar beliefs that I'd held in the new age, so I felt comfortable exploring them. It wasn't until I'd studied the whole Bible that I realized that my old new age methods and deliverance ministries shared similar unbiblical do-it-yourself theatrical methods.

Yet in those early days of my salvation, I didn't know any better. So, I listened to deliverance ministry YouTube videos, which recited prayers purportedly to cast out demons. Actually, these "prayers" were more like demands and commands to God which shocked me. The videos also commanded demons to leave in Jesus' name. I played these videos around the clock in my home, yet the spiritual warfare seemed to grow stronger.

I bought books of prayers that the author said would "rout out demons," and these prayers also consisted of commanding demons to leave "in Jesus' name." Still, the spiritual warfare increased, and the insomnia wore me down.

So, I purchased a session with a deliverance minister, who proceeded to wave a cross in front of me while yelling at demons to get out of me in Jesus' name. It was at that point that my eyes were opened and I realized the futility of these do-it-yourself methods. Yes, Jesus gave the disciples authority to cast out demons, but I realized that *authority* wasn't the issue. It was about what was wise, effective, and spiritually safe.

This book is a compilation of what I've learned about spiritual warfare through my daily Bible study, while earning a master's degree in seminary, while interviewing theologians for my YouTube channel,

INTRODUCTION

and in talking with women who've wrestled with spiritual warfare after they were saved out of deception.

I pray that this book will offer you a practical application guide to what the Bible teaches us about spiritual warfare.

All glory to God,
Doreen

Chapter 1: The Armor We Need

"Finally, be strengthened by the Lord and by his vast strength. Put on the full Armor of God so that you can stand against the tactics of the devil." Ephesians 6:10-13

Is there a sense that the enemy's trying to rob you of sleep, peace, and joy? Do you feel like you're oppressed by demonic forces? Praise the Lord that you that you don't have to face these spiritual warfare struggles alone.

When we talk about "spiritual warfare," we're not talking about something we can physically see. Spiritual warfare is the constant battle happening in the unseen realm. It's the age-old battle between good and evil, between the Kingdom of God and the forces of darkness. It's something we all face as Christians. Yet, the good news is that God has given us *everything* we need to stand strong against the devil's schemes.

God gave us the Bible to equip us in every matter, including spiritual warfare. In Ephesians 6:10-18, we read about a real and necessary truth: we need to put on the Armor of God every day. Without the Armor of God, you're walking into battle without protection. In this book we'll examine what the Bible says about the Armor of God, so you'll know what it is and how to put it on for spiritual protection.

Ephesians 6:13 says, "Therefore, take up the full Armor of God, so that you may be able to resist in the evil day, and having prepared everything, to take your stand." God isn't asking us to "suit up" alone. He's giving us the strength to withstand whatever comes our way. When you put on the Armor of God, you're actively participating in God's divine strength, not your own.

In this book, we'll look at the elements of the Armor of God, so you can see what the Bible says and how to apply it to your daily life:

1. **The Belt of Truth** (Ephesians 6:14)

Belts fasten everything together for soldiers, including strapping in their ammunition. Putting on the Belt of Truth means that you're firm in your knowledge of God's truth because you study the Bible. God's truth is the foundation for your decisions and actions, which helps to keep you on the straight and narrow path away from deception. The devil is the father of lies, and his goal is to deceive you, distort reality, discourage you, and make you question God's promises. The truth of God's Word is your protection. When you face lies from the enemy - whether it's questioning your purpose, or your identity - hold tightly to the truth of who you are in Christ. If you've repented, believe the Gospel, and have put your trust in Jesus Christ as your Lord and Savior, then you're adopted into God's family and your identity is a child of God.

2. **The Breastplate of Righteousness** (Ephesians 6:14)

A breastplate is designed to protect the heart during battles. After you were saved, God gave you a new heart that desires to be obedient to God and to live righteously (Ezekiel 11:19-20,36:26-27;2 Corinthians 5:17;John 3:3-6;Romans 6:4;Hebrews 8:10). Your righteousness doesn't come from your own works, but from Christ. This armor protects your new heart. If you're constantly battling guilt or shame, remember that Christ through His sacrifice covered you in His perfect righteousness.

3. **Shoes of the Gospel of Peace** (Ephesians 6:15)
Your shoes are meant to help you walk safely and firmly. The gospel is the message of peace. Shoes in the Armor of God are about having your feet ready and prepared to stand firm in battle, travel safely over rocky terrain, walk in obedience and righteousness to God, and spread the good news of the peace that only comes from the Gospel of Jesus Christ.

4. **The Shield of Faith** (Ephesians 6:16)
Soldiers are protected in battle with the shield they hold in front of themselves. The shield of faith is *your faith* in God's promises, sovereignty, and power. In the Armor of God, the shield of faith (your faith in God) stops and extinguishes the enemy's flaming arrows. When you stand firm in your faith in God, it's the equivalent of lifting up a shield in battle. Your faith in God is your defense against the enemy's tactics.

5. **The Helmet of Salvation** (Ephesians 6:17)
In battle, a soldier wears a helmet to protect his head from injury. In the Armor of God, the helmet of salvation protects your mind from the enemy's lies. The Bible calls the devil "the accuser" because he tries to discourage Christians. The Bible also says that the devil is "the father of lies" and "the author of confusion" because he lies and tries to confuse Christians. So protecting your mind from spiritual warfare is essential. You put on the helmet of salvation through your assurance that God saved you. If you genuinely have repented for your sins, believe the Gospel and have put your faith in the *real* Jesus (not a false unbiblical teaching about Jesus), and Jesus is your Lord and Savior, then Jesus

is holding you tightly. This assurance protects you when the enemy attempts to trigger doubt.

6. **The Sword of the Spirit** (Ephesians 6:17)

The sword of the Spirit in the Armor of God refers to God's Word, the Bible. Jesus used the Word when He was tempted in the wilderness (Mattew 4:1-11). He didn't argue with the devil; He quoted Scripture. When you face temptation or discouragement, you can use God's Word to cut through the lies and bring truth into the situation. This is the offensive weapon you have, which is one more reason why it's essential to read the Bible daily.

Spiritual warfare is real and it affects every Christian to varying degrees, yet God has equipped us with everything we need to stand firm. And not just stand, but to be victorious.

Reflection Questions:

1. Which piece of the Armor of God do you feel you need to focus upon the most right now? Why?

2. Have you ever experienced spiritual warfare through thoughts or feelings of fear, doubt, or anxiety? How did you respond?

3. In what areas of your life do you need to apply the truth of God's Word more consistently?

4. How can you make wearing the Armor of God a daily practice in your life?

Chapter 2: The Indwelling Holy Spirit

The moment that we're saved by God's grace and mercy through our faith in Jesus, the Holy Spirit indwells us. We become temples of the Holy Spirit. The Holy Spirit is our Comforter and Advocate who reminds us of Jesus' teachings. The indwelling Holy Spirit assures us that we *cannot* be possessed by demons. Why? Because the Holy Spirit, the very presence of God Himself, takes up residence within us. There's no room for darkness where the light of God dwells.

1 John 4:4 says, "Little children, you are from God and have overcome them, for he who is in you is greater than he who is in the world." The One who lives inside you is greater than any power of the enemy. The Holy Spirit is a guarantee of our security in Christ, and no force of darkness can overpower Him.

When you gave your life to Jesus, the Holy Spirit came to dwell inside of you. The Holy Spirit has sealed all believers, keeping them secure and shielded from demonic possession. Only unsaved people and false converts (those who claim to be a Christian but actually aren't) can have demons possession inside of them. Genuine Christians who've repented and believe the Gospel, and who've put their faith and trust in Jesus Christ for salvation, can't be possessed. The indwelling Holy Spirit won't allow demons to co-exist with Him.

While we, as believers, can never be *possessed* by demons, we can be

CHAPTER 2: THE INDWELLING HOLY SPIRIT

oppressed. Oppression is different from possession. Possession means total control from within, and a complete takeover. Oppression is more like a heavy weight from the outside, and an ongoing battle that tries to wear us down. It's a subtle and often persistent attack where the enemy seeks to discourage, confuse, or distract us.

Oppression may make you feel overwhelmed by the struggles of life, the lies of the enemy, and the pressure to become discouraged. That feeling of being weighed down, like something is pushing against you from all sides, can be demonic oppression. This is called "The Spirit of Heaviness" in Isaiah 61:3 KJV and it can be exchanged for the Garment of Praise, or sincerely praising God for His glorious goodness in your life.

Yet in those vulnerable moments when you're tired, hungry, or someone has disappointed you, the enemy pounces. The Bible says that we need to stay alert and sober-minded because Satan is like a roaring lion seeking someone to devour (1 Peter 5:8).

The enemy tries to take advantage of vulnerable people by whispering lies that you're not enough, that you're failing, or that God has abandoned you. These are examples of spiritual oppression. The enemy may not possess your soul, but he will try to attack your mind, your emotions, and your spirit to discourage your evangelism and your walk with God. He's desperately trying to stop the spread of the Gospel, and to thwart more people believing in Jesus. Yet, God is not mocked!

Praise the Lord that this battle isn't one you have to face alone. You're never alone and never without help. The Holy Spirit lives within you. And He's always ready to equip you, to help you resist the enemy's tactics, and to protect your heart and mind. You don't have to fear the enemy's oppression in spiritual warfare, because when you cry out in prayer, Christ will give you the strength to stand firm in your faith.

Ephesians 6:10-13 encourages us to "be strong in the Lord and in the power of His might" and to put on the full Armor of God so that we can stand against the schemes of the devil. The Armor of God shields us from the oppressive attacks that seek to drain our strength, faith, peace, and joy.

The enemy's oppression seeks to wear us down. Yet with each piece of the Armor - truth, righteousness, peace, faith, salvation, and the Word of God - we have everything we need to fight back. The enemy may try to bombard your mind with lies or make you feel overwhelmed, but you have weapons to resist. And those weapons are mighty through God (2 Corinthians 10:4). You're *never* alone or defenseless.

The power to stand against oppression comes not from your own strength but from the Holy Spirit Who is within you. He helps you recognize when you're under attack and then He gives you the discernment to know how to resist the lies of the enemy.

Romans 8:11 says, "And if the Spirit of him who raised Jesus from the dead lives in you, then he who raised Christ from the dead will also bring your mortal bodies to life through his Spirit who lives in you." The amazing power of the Holy Spirit is at work within you! You don't have to endure battles alone since the Holy Spirit is within you.

I've found that one of the most powerful ways to resist oppression is through prayer. When the heaviness of life threatens to overwhelm me, I turn to God in prayer. As mentioned earlier, sincerely praising God is putting on the Garment of Praise in exchange for the oppressive Spirit of Heaviness (Isaiah 61:3 KJV). Think of everything that you're grateful to God for, especially your salvation. Praise God for His goodness!

The enemy's attacks are meant to discourage and defeat you, but with the Holy Spirit living within you, you can't be swayed (Romans 8:37). Don't allow the enemy to steal your peace or your joy. Remember that the battle is already won. Jesus has defeated the enemy once and for all.

So, as you face the spiritual battles in your life, don't forget that you're protected. *Christians can't be possessed* because with the indwelling Holy Spirit standing guard. You will face oppression with demons outside of you harassing you, but never with demons inside of you. With God's help, you'll be able to resist the devil's schemes, and rest peacefully in Christ.

Reflection Questions:

1. In what ways have you experienced spiritual oppression? How did you respond?
2. How does reading the Bible daily help to remind you of the indwelling Holy Spirit, so you can stay reassured during spiritual battles?
3. If you're normally a do-it-yourself person, how can you learn to trust that God hears your prayers and will fight your spiritual battles?
4. How can you encourage a friend who may be feeling spiritually oppressed and give her Biblical guidance about how to handle spiritual warfare?

Sister, you're never alone in the fight. The Holy Spirit is within you, ready to help you stand against any attack. You're secure in Christ, and He can overcome any oppression the enemy throws your way. Keep your eyes fixed upon Him and remember: He is with you always.

Chapter 3: Trusting Jesus to Fight the Battle

If you're someone who's used to doing everything yourself, or if you have control or trust issues, you may believe that you need to take charge and use your authority to fight against the devil. You imagine yourself as Buffy the Vampire Slayer or Joan of Arc chasing demons away in Jesus' name. After all, we've been given authority in Christ, right? And Jesus did say we have power over the enemy (Luke 10:19). So, what's the big deal about directly commanding the devil to leave?

When you feel attacked, it can be a knee-jerk reaction to try to solve the problem yourself. You feel the pressure, the anxiety, the weight, and you think, "I need to step up and tell the devil to go away!" You recall the movies of exorcists commanding Satan to leave, or the theatrical deliverance ministry videos. And in the heat of the moment, we may temporarily forget that Jesus is with us always.

There's a reason why the Bible encourages us to always rely on Jesus, especially in the fight against spiritual forces. The truth is, it's spiritually dangerous and unwise to get in the boxing ring with the devil and try to command him to leave. Why would the personification of evil who hates humanity listen to us, even if we add the tagline, "In Jesus' name"? The devil may pretend to leave us alone, but then he'll return with his demon buddies because he doesn't respect humanity. Again, this is not

CHAPTER 3: TRUSTING JESUS TO FIGHT THE BATTLE

about whether Jesus gave you *authority*. It's about being wise.

The New Testament contains "epistles" or letters to the early church written by the apostles. These epistles are instructions for all believers. *None of the epistles instruct Christians to cast out demons.* Not one! Instead, the epistles give us instructions for how to protect ourselves from spiritual warfare, as we'll examine in this book.

We don't fight against flesh and blood, but against rulers, authorities, and powers of darkness (Ephesians 6:12). The devil is crafty, and do we *really* believe that he'll obey a human's commands, even if that person says, "In Jesus' name"? No, the devil will scheme another way to attack the human, because the devil only obeys direct orders from God, as we see in the book of Job.

We can also see in Acts 19:13-16 where people were invoking the name of Jesus to try to cast out demons. But the demon that was possessing an unsaved man responded, "Jesus I know, and Paul I recognize, but who are you?" The man possessed with the demon then attacked them, and they fled from the house naked and wounded.

Why did this happen? The exorcists acted in their own strength, and it didn't end well. This story is a warning. It shows us that it's not enough to just use the name of Jesus like some magic formula. There's a reason why we need to rely upon Jesus, not ourselves, to cast out demons.

The devil has been around a lot longer than us, and he knows how to deceive, confuse, and even intimidate. Commanding the devil is like sending a child into battle, when the King has offered to go.

Jesus Himself shows us the way. When He was tempted in the wilderness by the devil, He said, "it is written" and quoted the Bible. There's no record in this account of Jesus yelling or engaging in deliverance ministry theatrics. Jesus responded to the devil with God's Word. We too need to rely upon the Bible's instructions for how to deal with spiritual warfare.

Spiritual warfare is not something to approach with pride or self-reliance. Ephesians 6:10-11 tells us, "Be strengthened by the Lord and by His vast strength. Put on the full Armor of God so that you can stand against the schemes of the devil." Notice that we're strengthened by *His strength*, not our own. When we act out of our own confidence, we're not leaning on the one thing that gives us true power: Jesus.

Don't talk one-on-one with the devil or demons. Cry out to Jesus to help you when you're in a battle, and He'll be there.

Deliverance ministries are a big profitable industry, and they don't like critics of their money-making business. So, they claim that critics are filled with a "religious spirit" (which is a made-up fabricated term that isn't in the Bible). Or they claim that critics are blaspheming the Holy Spirit, when that phrase applies only to those who reject the Gospel.

Please be discerning and compare everything to Scripture (Acts 17:11).

The Bible calls us to *resist* the enemy (James 4:7) not to fight him. We rely upon Jesus and put on the full Armor of God. Jesus is the one who defeated the enemy once and for all on the cross, and He's the one who fights for us now. We don't need to prove anything to the enemy or show off our own strength. We need to submit to God and rely upon the One who won the victory.

Reflection Questions:

1. Do you struggle with submitting to God, or trusting Him?
2. Have you prayed for help with any control or trust issues you struggle with? Do these issues make you want to do everything yourself? Do you have difficulty trusting in God's plans and timing?
3. What area of your life are you trying to manage by yourself instead of praying for God's help?
4. How can you remember to pray for God's help during spiritual battles?Sister, the battle is real, but the victory is already won. Don't try to fight in your own strength. Trust Jesus as your King,

CHAPTER 3: TRUSTING JESUS TO FIGHT THE BATTLE

and rest in knowing that He's already defeated the enemy.

Chapter 4: Resisting the Devil

"Submit therefore to God. Resist the devil, and he will flee from you. Draw near to God and He will draw near to you." James 4:7-8

Spiritual warfare isn't like exorcism movies with dramatic battles in plain view. The devil is sneakier and more subtle than that. He wages war against Christians through offering temptations, by whispering discouragement, and harassing you when you're trying to sleep. Now, the devil isn't like God, so he isn't omnipresent (everywhere) or omniscient (all-knowing). He is, however, pure evil who has studied humanity for thousands of years. His goal is to compete with God to "win" as many souls as possible and lure them into his lair of eternal torment.

Have you ever noticed how quickly the devil can attack you when you're exhausted, emotionally vulnerable, or after you've just shared the Gospel with someone? Yet, it's futile to rely upon our own strength or willpower to resist the enemy.

The first part of James 4:7 tells us to "submit therefore to God." Submission isn't a word we often like to hear. It feels like giving up control, doesn't it? But submitting to God means acknowledging that

CHAPTER 4: RESISTING THE DEVIL

He knows better than we do. It's trusting in the Lord with all our heart (Proverbs 3:5). Submission means that you realize that God's will is superior to our limited human knowledge.

Submission also means obedience to God's Word. Now, this isn't *legalism* which means believing that you're saved by your good works, when the Bible clearly says we're saved by God's grace and mercy. Once we're saved, God gives us a new heart that desires to please God. Obedience isn't the *cause* of being saved, but a *result* of being saved.

The second sentence of James 4:7 is equally important: "Resist the devil and he will flee." The devil is like a house burglar looking for easy marks. A home with a gate, guard dogs, and security lights and cameras will be passed by in favor of homes with no security. Similarly, the devil flees from Christians who are submissive and obedient to God, because that means they won't succumb to the devil's traps and temptations.

Resisting the devil means standing firm in our faith in God's strength (not trying to use willpower or our own strength). As the next verse James 4:8 proclaims: "Draw near to God and He will draw near to you." The enemy wants to isolate you, to separate you from the source of your strength. When you're in the midst of a struggle, do you find yourself pulling away from God or drawing closer to Him?

Let's get honest. It's tempting to feel distant from God when you're discouraged or overwhelmed. Yet, God calls us to draw near to Him. That's where our strength comes from.

Drawing near to God isn't a physical or emotional feeling. It's a decision to immerse yourself in Bible study and fervent prayer. You may not *feel* God's presence, yet you can *trust* that He's there.

In spiritual warfare, one of the most powerful things you can do is turn to God in the middle of the battle. Prayer, worship, and immersing yourself in His Word are the tools that draw you near to Him and help you resist the enemy. When you're feeling weak, remind yourself of God's promises. Read them out loud from His Word.

By staying grounded in daily Bible study, and leaning upon God for strength, we're able to submit to God and resist the devil. Trust God's promise that the devil will flee!

Reflection Questions:

1. Have you recently struggled with any temptations? How did you resist them?
2. In what ways are you more obedient to God, compared to before you were saved?
3. How can you arrange your schedule so that you're sure to read the Bible daily?
4. What changes do you need to make to help you resist the devil (such as avoiding certain locations or people)?

Chapter 5: Firm in Your Faith

"Be sober-minded; be watchful. Your adversary the devil prowls around like a roaring lion, seeking someone to devour. Resist him, firm in your faith, knowing that the same kinds of suffering are being experienced by your brotherhood throughout the world."
1 Peter 5:8-9

Have you ever felt like you're struggling all alone, and that no one understands how you feel nor offers to help? Perhaps you're ashamed to admit your situation to others. Feeling lonely or being isolated can be a tactic of the devil in spiritual warfare.

All Christians face spiritual battles including fear, temptation, loneliness, or doubt. The devil may try to divide us and make us feel isolated, but the truth is that we are part of a universal family of believers headed by Christ. We're not alone.

The key to standing firm is faith. The enemy's biggest strategy is to attack your faith and try to make you question God's goodness, His plan for your life, or even His very existence. This is where the battle begins: in our hearts and minds. When you feel the weight of doubt, fear, or discouragement, that's when the enemy's trying to devour you.

In 1 Peter 5:9, we're called to "resist him, firm in your faith." Not in your own strength, not in your own wisdom, but in your faith in God.

Standing firm in your faith doesn't mean that you won't face struggles; it means that even in the face of struggles, you'll hold on to the truth that God is bigger than your circumstances. It means refusing to let the enemy's lies shake your trust in God. Instead of allowing fear or doubt to control you, you choose to trust God. The more that you study the Bible, the more you'll learn about God and the more that you'll trust Him.

Think about the roaring lion image that Peter uses. In biblical times, a lion was a real threat to shepherds and travelers. Comparing the devil to a roaming deadly creature conveys the urgency of resisting his evil plans. We need to be alert and sober-minded to avoid the devil's traps.

By the way, "sober-minded" doesn't necessarily mean abstinence from alcohol. The Bible says that drunkenness is a sin, which would also include intoxication from drugs. I've been sober without any alcohol or intoxication since 2004; however, I don't think there's anything wrong with Christians enjoying a glass of wine unless it leads to drunkenness. You can imagine how the devil takes advantage of those who abuse drugs or alcohol.

Praise Jesus for crushing the power of the enemy on the cross! As a believer, you're sealed in the Holy Spirit and Jesus is with you always. We turn to God's promises and reassurances in His Word such as 2 Thessalonians 3:3, "But the Lord is faithful, and He will strengthen you and protect you from the evil one."

One of the best ways we build our faith is through daily reading the Bible. The more you read and meditate on God's Word, the more your faith grows. And when your faith grows, you're more equipped to stand firm against the devil's lies.

Reflection Questions:

CHAPTER 5: FIRM IN YOUR FAITH

1. When do you notice that your faith is the strongest? What factors boost your faith? What factors (that you can avoid) tend to shred your faith?
2. Which Bible books or passages do you turn to, when you need your faith replenished?
3. Can you think of a time when the enemy tried to discourage you with accusations or reminders of your sinful past? How did you handle this?
4. What can you say to a friend who may be struggling with her faith?Standing firm in faith isn't always easy, but it's always worth it

Chapter 6: Take Every Thought Captive

"For though we walk in the flesh, we do not war according to the flesh. For the weapons of our warfare aren't carnal but mighty in God for pulling down strongholds, casting down arguments and every high thing that exalts itself against the knowledge of God, bringing every thought into captivity to the obedience of Christ." 2 Corinthians 10:3-5

Spiritual warfare doesn't always look like a dramatic confrontation with an enemy. It often starts with our thoughts. The devil loves to target your mind because he knows that if he can influence your thoughts, he can control your actions. What you think about affects how you feel, and how you feel drives your behavior. So if the enemy can manipulate your thoughts, he can try to lead you down a destructive path.

Let's take a closer look at 2 Corinthians 10:3-5 which reminds us that our warfare is spiritual, not physical. The devil tries to defeat Christians with strongholds such as temptations to sin, being confused by false gospel teachings, and discouragement.

In the same spiritual vein, God equips believers with spiritual weapons

CHAPTER 6: TAKE EVERY THOUGHT CAPTIVE

against these spiritual warfare battles. Through God's mighty power, these weapons break down the devil's strongholds. This doesn't mean that we are to rush into battle against the devil, which would be unwise like a child battling a raging wild beast. All battles are fought by God.

If we've been unknowingly deceived by false teachings, God can pull down these strongholds as we bring our thinking under the control of Christ's authority and truth. We are to "take every thought captive," which means being sober-minded, alert, and comparing every teaching and thought to Scripture so we won't be deceived.

So, when the devil accuses us to try to discourage us, we must remember that these aren't thoughts from God. These are lies from the enemy designed to pull us away from the truth of who we are in Christ. We don't have to accept every thought that comes into our minds.

The Bible says that we have the power, through God, to "cast down arguments and every high thing that exalts itself against the knowledge of God." In other words, we have the authority to reject every thought that doesn't align with God's truth. That strength comes from God, and the ability to discern false teachings from true comes from daily Bible study and prayer.

As Romans 12:2 says, "And do not be conformed to this world, but be transformed by the renewing of your mind, so that you may prove what the will of God is, that which is good and acceptable and perfect."

This verse speaks to the inward renewal of your mind that comes from daily Bible study and prayer, which brings your thoughts into alignment with God's will. Through this process, false teachings and the enemy's lies are instantly recognized as sour notes to be ignored and discarded.

One practical way to do this is by taking those negative, destructive thoughts and replacing them with God's Word. When the enemy tells you that you're not enough, God's Word says that you're fearfully and wonderfully made (Psalm 139:14). When you feel like you're hopeless,

God's Word says that you're complete in Christ (Colossians 2:10).

When you're overwhelmed with fear, God's Word tells you that He hasn't given you a spirit of fear, but of power, love, and a sound mind (2 Timothy 1:7). Of course, it's not about our own competence or worth, but about what our sinless Lord and Savior Jesus did for us on the cross.

When you take your thoughts captive, your mind is more at peace. You stop letting the enemy dictate what you think, and you let God's truth rule your thoughts. When the enemy's lies start to rise up about your past sins or your identity, hold them up to the truth of God's Word. Reject the lies and choose to focus upon whatever is true, pure, and lovely (c.f., Philippians 4:8).

Reflection Questions:

1. What false teachings have you rejected, because you've compared them to the Bible?
2. Do you ever have moments when you fear that God doesn't love you, or that you're not "good enough" for God to use you for His service? What are ways to combat these accusations from the devil, instead of succumbing to this spiritual warfare?
3. What specific Scriptures can you memorize to combat the lies of the enemy when they come?
4. When you feel overwhelmed by hurtful thoughts, how can you shift your focus to God's truth?

Remember, guarding your mind is an ongoing process. You'll have to take every thought captive again and again. But with God's Word as your weapon, you can stand firm in the truth and walk in the peace that only He can give. Don't let the enemy have a foothold in your mind, dear sister! Stay in God's Word, stand firm in faith, and pray always.

Chapter 7: The Shield of Faith

"In all circumstances take up the shield of faith, with which you can extinguish all the flaming darts of the evil one." Ephesians 6:16

Spiritual warfare isn't fought with physical weapons, but with prayers, Bible study, the Gospel and faith. The enemy comes at us in unexpected ways, often targeting our insecurities, our doubts, and our fears. Praise God for giving us a shield that can extinguish all of the enemy's attacks!

In physical battles, soldiers use shields to protect themselves from projectiles as a physical barrier between themselves and the enemy. Shields keep them safe from harm.

In the same way, the shield of faith works as a barrier between us and the attacks of the enemy. Faith protects us by reminding us of God's truth, His promises, and His power. When the enemy launches his fiery darts - doubts, fears, temptations, lies - we can raise our shield of faith, blocking those attacks and standing firm in God's strength.

Notice that the Bible tells us to take up the shield of faith "in all circumstances." It's an active choice on our part. When you face struggles, whether it's an unexpected challenge at work, a tough relationship, or a health scare, do you choose to pick up your shield of faith? Or do you let fear or doubt overtake you? It's an obvious choice.

Faith is the key to standing firm against the enemy's attacks. The enemy wants to get us to doubt God's sovereignty, power, and goodness. He wants us to question whether God really has our best interests at heart. The devil wants to wedge into your relationship with God, by discouraging and disheartening you.

This isn't about the world's messages to "have faith in yourself." This is one-hundred percent about having faith in God. Our salvation rests in Jesus' righteousness, not our own. The devil attacks us to try to lessen our faith in God. The devil also hopes to make us doubt our ability to share the Gospel and make disciples as Jesus commanded of all believers in The Great Commission. Yet our evangelism rests upon God's strength, not our own. So the devil really has no legitimate arguments.

That's why raising your shield of faith means to combat Satan's lies with God's truth. If your faith waivers because you're enduring harsh trials, turn to God's Word. Read or listen to audios of the Bible. Pray fervently for God to increase your hope, encouragement, and faith. Remember that God's plans are much better than our own, so He may answer your prayers about your current circumstances in ways that initially disappoint you. This can be God's testing or steering you in a better direction.

Shadrach, Meshach, and Abednego were thrown into a fiery furnace because they refused to worship the king's golden idol. Yet, their faith in God was unshakable. They said, "If this be so, our God whom we serve is able to deliver us from the burning fiery furnace, and He will deliver us out of your hand, O king. But if not, be it known to you, O king, that we will not serve your gods or worship the golden image that you have set up" (Daniel 3:17-18). Their shield of faith protected them from the fear and pressure that surrounded them. Jesus showed up as the fourth person in the furnace, protecting them in a powerful way.

In the same way, our faith acts as a shield that protects us from the attacks of the enemy. But this shield doesn't just protect us; it also extinguishes the enemy's fiery darts. The Bible says that the shield of faith can "extinguish all the flaming darts of the evil one." The enemy shoots fiery darts at us such as temptations, accusations, and fears. These darts may come in the form of lies like, "You're not good enough," "Your past sins are unforgiveable," or "God doesn't care about you." The enemy's fiery darts may come as fears about your future or your competency. But when we raise the shield of faith, those darts can't penetrate. Faith blocks them out as the devil's lies bounce off the shield.

The more we raise our shield of faith, the more of an automatic reflex this action becomes. The more we stand on God's Word and choose to believe, the more we learn to trust Him. And the more we trust Him, the stronger our faith.

It's encouraging to read the list of heroes of faith in Hebrews 11. This "great cloud of witnesses" (Hebrews 12:1) refers to the men and women described in Hebrews 11, who encourage us to continue pressing on and having faith in the Lord.

Reflection Questions:

1. What firey darts from the enemy have you encountered? How did your faith in God help to shield you from these darts?
2. Have you noticed that your faith in God increases when you review the ways that He has helped you?
3. How can you stay encouraged to remain strong in your faith, during seasons of suffering and trials?
4. What are some ways to remind yourself to lift up the shield of faith when attacks occur?

Faith is a powerful shield that you can wield every day. Whenever fear arises and doubts creep in, remember that you have a shield to protect you. Everyone's faith waivers occasionally, so please don't judge yourself if you need help from God, prayer, and Bible study to boost your faith. He will help you when you turn to Him.

Chapter 8: The Helmet of Salvation

"And take the helmet of salvation, and the sword of the Spirit, which is the word of God." Ephesians 6:17

The helmet is a piece of armor that protects the head, which is one of our most vulnerable areas. As we've been discussing, your mind is the enemy's chief target in his quest to discourage and confuse you. That's why the helmet of salvation is essential in protecting you from spiritual warfare. The helmet of salvation guards our minds, giving us the assurance of God's sovereignty and protecting us from the lies of the enemy.

The helmet of salvation reminds us that Jesus' work on the cross was finished. Those who trust in Jesus are secure. This protection covers and protects us from the enemy's attacks on our identity, our faith, and our future. The enemy tries to attack our minds with accusations like, "You're not really saved," or "You've messed up too much for God to still love you." But the helmet of salvation defends against these lies, reminding us of the truth of our identity in Christ.

Salvation is the only way that our sins are forgiven, so that we're reconciled with God and can abide in Christ.1 Thessalonians 5:8 says,

"But let us, who are of the day, be sober, putting on the breastplate of faith and love, and as a helmet, the hope of salvation." Notice how the Bible connects *salvation* with *hope*. When you wear the helmet of salvation, you're embracing a hope that goes beyond the circumstances of today. It's the hope of eternal life in Christ, and the hope of being united with Him forever.

The helmet of salvation is the result of prayer and daily Bible study to know that you were saved by God's grace and mercy, through your faith in Jesus as your Lord and Savior. This knowledge makes the devil's accusations bounce off your helmet. You know that the devil is lying, because you know Who Jesus is and what He did for you on the cross. Just like if someone accused you of being a purple elephant, you'd roll your eyes because you know that's untrue. You don't live in fear or insecurity, because your identity is secure in Christ. Praise God that our salvation is based upon His grace!

The helmet of salvation reminds us that Jesus defeated death and sin through His sacrifice on our behalf and His subsequent resurrection. The enemy will try to find a weak spot in our faith, yet we hold fast in trusting in the Gospel of Jesus Christ. It's not about whether we're strong enough to sustain the enemy's attacks. It's about what Jesus has already done on the cross.

When we wear the helmet of salvation, we walk in the victory that Jesus has secured for us. This means we needn't fear the enemy's attacks because we know the outcome of the battle. Jesus is our champion, and we safely abide in Him.

The enemy tries to plant doubts in our mind about past sins and our current situations. Yet we already know that our sins *were* bad, and that they were forgiven by Jesus' sacrifice the moment that we believed. We know we were wretched sinners before we were saved by God's grace. The enemy can't add to this knowledge. When we keep our eyes upon Jesus instead of on self-pity or self-obsession, we wear the helmet of

CHAPTER 8: THE HELMET OF SALVATION

salvation that protects our mind from the enemy's attacks.

Reflection Questions:

1. What lies has the enemy tried to accuse you of? How did you handle this?
2. What steps do you take if you ever doubt God's love for you or your salvation?
3. How can you stay focused upon Jesus during your trials or in seasons of suffering?
4. Have you ever had someone accuse you of something that you knew you were innocent of? What did you do in response to these accusations?

Wearing the helmet of salvation is more than just a symbol. It's a daily choice to remind yourself of the security you have in Christ. When the enemy tries to attack your mind with lies, doubts, or insecurities, raise that helmet high. You don't have to live in fear or uncertainty as long as you continue to abide in Jesus. Keep your mind fixed on this truth, and the enemy's lies will lose their power.

Chapter 9: The Breastplate of Righteousness

"Stand firm therefore, having girded your loins with truth, and having put on the breastplate of righteousness." Ephesians 6:14

The breastplate was an important piece of armor for soldiers, as it protected the chest, heart and lungs. In the same way, the breastplate of righteousness protects our hearts and keeps us spiritually alive and strong.

Proverbs 4:23 tells us, "Above all else, guard your heart, for everything you do flows from it." The enemy knows that if he can attack our hearts emotionally and spiritually, he can knock us off course. But when we wear the breastplate of righteousness, our hearts are protected against the lies, guilt, and shame that the enemy tries to use to bring us down.

But what does the "breastplate of righteousness" really mean? It's not about our own righteousness; it's about the righteousness of Christ. When we place our trust in Jesus, we're clothed in His righteousness. 2 Corinthians 5:21 says, "For our sake he made him to be sin who knew no sin, so that in him we might become the righteousness of God." When God the Father looks at us, He doesn't see our sin. He sees the righteousness of Jesus the Son, and that righteousness is what protects our hearts from the accusations and attacks of the enemy.

CHAPTER 9: THE BREASTPLATE OF RIGHTEOUSNESS

It's easy to fall into the trap of thinking we need to earn righteousness by doing good works or following the rules. After all, this world is built upon being productive and accomplishing as much a possible. However, any righteousness which Jesus imparted to us on the cross is a gift of God's love. Knowing this truth guards our hearts.

Of course, we still need to be obedient and walk the straight and narrow path with Jesus. We do this not to earn salvation, but because we're grateful for our salvation. Jesus said, "If you love me, obey my commandments" (John 14:15). Jesus clothed us in His righteousness to save us and deliver us from sin. At the moment that God saved us, we were given a new heart that desires to please God and be obedient.

All Christians still sin occasionally (Romans 3:23; 1 John 1:8); however, the indwelling Holy Spirit convicts our sin. Before salvation, we didn't care about pleasing or obeying God. But as Christian women, our hearts hurt when we realize we've sinned, so we repent and pray for God to direct our paths away from sin. So even when we fall short (which we all do), the breastplate of righteousness protects our hearts. Romans 8:1 says: "There is therefore now no condemnation for those who are in Christ Jesus." When the enemy tries to accuse us, we can stand firm in the truth that we're forgiven and accepted by God, not because of what we've done but because of what Jesus has done for us.

When we wear the breastplate of righteousness, we can stand with confidence before God, knowing we are clothed in Jesus' righteousness. We don't have to let the enemy drag us down with guilt or shame. Our hearts are protected by the truth that we are righteous in Christ.

The breastplate also guards us from emotional attacks. The enemy attempts to attack our hearts with discouragement, bitterness, unforgiveness, and anger. He tries to lead us away from God's peace. But when we wear the breastplate of righteousness, we're able to reject those emotions and walk in God's peace. Colossians 3:15 tells us, "Let the peace of Christ rule in your hearts, to which indeed you were called in one body. And be thankful."

Reflection Questions:

1. Have you struggled with guilt or shame about your past? How did you overcome these painful emotions?
2. What is the importance in your life, of keeping your eyes upon Jesus and off of this world?
3. How does it help you to know that believers are clothed in Jesus' perfect righteousness?
4. Sometimes bitterness seems justified, yet it is painful and destructive. What are ways that you've let go of bitterness?

When the enemy attacks your heart with guilt, shame, or negativity, stand firm in the knowledge that Jesus cloaked believers in His righteousness on the cross.

Chapter 10: The Belt of Truth

"Stand, therefore, with truth like a belt around your waist."
Ephesians 6:14

The belt was another essential piece of battle equipment for soldiers. The belt held together the pieces of armor, including their sword, keeping everything secure and in place. The belt of truth serves the same purpose in our spiritual armor. It's what fastens everything together. Without truth, everything else falls apart. The belt of truth is the foundation based upon the truth of Who God is and what He's promised us.

God is the source of truth, and truth is one of God's defining attributes. Jesus Himself said, "I am the way, the truth, and the life" (John 14:6). So, truth isn't just God's knowledge and wisdom; it's His essence. When we put on the belt of truth, we're securing and anchoring ourselves in God. After all, God can't contradict Himself or lie (Titus 1:2), and His truth is unchanging and transcendent. God is the Creator and His Word the Bible is true (John 17:17).

In contrast, the devil is the father of lies (John 8:44) and the author of confusion (1 Corinthians 14:33). He purposely twists truth to plant seeds of doubt in Christians. In the Garden of Eden, he used half-truths by asking Eve, "Did God actually say, 'You shall not eat of any tree in the garden'?" (Genesis 3:1). This was a distortion of God's command. The devil twisted the truth enough to make Eve question what she knew to be true about God's character. The enemy still does the same thing today. He tries to get us to question God's Word, to make us doubt what God has said by repeating unfounded lies such as saying the Bible is mistranslated or that it has missing books.

But when we're rooted in the truth of God's Word, we easily recognize those lies. Like the Bereans of Acts 17:11, we compare everything to Scripture as our measurement of truth. We quickly spot the distortions the enemy tries to feed us. When the enemy says, "You're not good enough," we instead stand firmly upon the truth of God's Word, which says we are fearfully and wonderfully made (Psalm 139:14). When the enemy whispers, "God has abandoned you," we hold to the truth that He will never leave us nor forsake us (Deuteronomy 31:6). The belt of truth helps us recognize and reject the lies.

When the enemy tried to trick Jesus in the wilderness, He fought back with the truth of Scripture: "It is written" (Matthew 4:1-11). This is why it's so important for us to know God's Word. The Bible isn't just a book to be read when we feel like it; it's our weapon, our shield, and our foundation. It's the truth that holds everything else together. When we know the truth of God's Word, we stand firm against the lies of the enemy and remain grounded in God's promises.

Of course, it's not enough to just know the truth intellectually. We also need to live by it. Jesus said, "If you abide in my word, you are truly my disciples, and you will know the truth, and the truth will set you free" (John 8:31-32). Abiding in God's Word means that the Bible is the foundation for how we view everything. This is called having a "Biblical worldview." When we live by God's truth, we're set free from the enemy's lies that try to entangle us, and free from the confusion and doubt that the enemy wants to sow.

CHAPTER 10: THE BELT OF TRUTH

Living by God's truth also means we must be willing to be honest with ourselves. Sometimes the enemy tries to deceive us into believing that we don't need to change. One of the enemy's big lies is that we can live sinfully, as long as it makes us happy. But when we embrace God's truth and study the Bible daily, we embrace the reality of who we are: sinners in need of repentance and God's grace. We realize the truth that we are the creation of a perfectly holy God Who expects us to sincerely strive to live holy lives.

The belt of truth holds everything together. Without it, we find ourselves vulnerable to the enemy's lies and confusion. But when we wrap ourselves in God's truth by studying the Bible, we stand strong. Truth shines the light of clarity to dispel the darkness.

Reflection Questions:

1. What lies have you heard about the Bible, and how did you counter these lies with truth?
2. How can reading the Bible daily help you to recognize false teachings?
3. Which Bible passages help you to feel calmer in the midst of trials?
4. How can prayer help you during moments of doubt or confusion?

Chapter 11: The Sword of the Spirit

"And take the helmet of salvation, and the sword of the Spirit, which is the word of God." Ephesians 6:17

The sword is a powerful weapon which soldiers used in battles to defend themselves, and also to attack the enemy. In the same way, the sword of the Spirit - God's Word, the Bible - is our weapon in spiritual warfare. But the Bible isn't just any weapon. It's a sharp, powerful, and living weapon as we read in Hebrews 4:12, "For the word of God is living and active and sharper than any two-edged sword…"

As the sword of the Spirit, the Bible isn't just a book we read occasionally or a verse we quote when we're feeling down. The Bible is the living, active Word of God, and it has the power to cut through the lies, doubts, and deceptions of the enemy. When we read, hear, and speak God's Word, we're wielding a sword that can defeat the enemy's attacks.

That's why we need to know the Bible, since you can't use a sword that you don't know how to wield. If you've never taken the time to read and meditate upon God's Word, it will be difficult to use it in the heat of battle. I was age 59 when I finally took the time to read the entire Bible and I regret that I didn't do so sooner.

Psalm 119:11 says, "Your word I have hidden in my heart, that I might not sin against You." This means that we need to tuck God's Word into our heart, and memorize verses that we can retrieve during battles for encouragement and spiritual protection. Listening to audios of the Bible is also helpful in memorizing Scripture.

When the enemy tries to convince us that we're alone in the battle, we can remind ourselves, "The Lord is with me; I will not fear" (Psalm 118:6).

The sword of the Spirit is also a weapon of offense. It's called the sword of the Spirit because it is the Holy Spirit equipping us with the God-breathed Bible (2 Timothy 3:16). When we face spiritual attacks, it's tempting to curl up into a fetal position and try to hide. Yet God calls us to take up the sword and move forward because the sword of the Spirit isn't just about defending ourselves; it's also about advancing.

God has called us to take His truth into the world, to share the Gospel of Jesus Christ, and to bring His light into dark places. The Gospel is the power of God for salvation for all who believe (Romans 1:16). As we stand strong in His Word and share it with others, we participate in the spiritual battle that is advancing the kingdom of God.

Reflection Questions:

1. Have you memorized any Scripture? Have you prayed for God to help you to memorize verses?
2. When the enemy attacks with lies and doubts, how can you use God's Word to resist and overcome him?
3. Have you prayed for opportunities, boldness, and courage to share the Gospel?
4. What are your favorite Bible verses? Have you committed them to

memory?

Chapter 12: The Shoes of the Gospel of Peace

"and having shod your feet with the preparation of the gospel of peace." Ephesians 6:15

The final piece of the Armor of God are the shoes of the Gospel of peace. Soldiers wore footwear during battle for protection and mobility. As Ephesians 6:15 reminds us, the spiritual shoes are for preparation to bring the Gospel to others. These shoes equip us for evangelism as a way to thwart the devil's schemes. They also protect us when we travel the rocky roads of trials. The Bible says this is the Gospel of peace, because through Jesus' sacrifice on the cross our sins were forgiven and the Holy Spirit indwelled us. True and lasting peace is a fruit of the Spirit (Galatians 5:22-23).

When I think about peace, I recall Jesus' words in John 14:27: "Peace I leave with you, My peace I give to you; not as the world gives do I give to you." It's easy to confuse the world's version of peace with the peace Jesus offers. The world's peace is often circumstantial, dependent on external factors such as relationships, finances, or health. Yet the peace of Christ transcends worldly circumstances. Only salvation through Jesus offers a peace that surpasses understanding, a peace that remains calm even in the chaos of life.

For me, this peace from salvation has been life-changing. Before God saved me, I chased "inner peace" through new age methods such as yoga, eastern meditation, and visualization. These methods made me feel "high" rather than peaceful, and even that sensation was temporary. Since being saved in 2017, I've endured a lot of trials and spiritual warfare. Yet amazingly, I've stayed peaceful through it all, especially in comparison to how I reacted to trials before salvation! This peace comes from within through the Holy Spirit.

I think about the disciples terrified by the storm on the sea of Galilee while Jesus calmly rebuked the wind and the waves and said, "Peace, be still" (Mark 4:35-41). God is sovereign, which is so reassuring when enduring the storms of life. We may not see a solution, or we may imagine a solution different from God's plans. The key to not getting upset during storms is to trust His will and His ways.

The shoes of peace also remind us that we can stand firm during battles. As women, we face unique challenges, but God's Word assures us that we're not called to fight alone. As Ephesians 6:15 says, we are to be prepared to go and share the Gospel of peace with others.

In Isaiah 52:7, we read, "How beautiful upon the mountains are the feet of him who brings good news, who proclaims peace, who brings glad tidings of good things…" As women, we're called to be bearers of this peace, spreading the message of Christ wherever we go. Our peace is not just for us; it's meant to overflow into the lives of those around us.

In Isaiah 26:3, God promises, "You will keep him in perfect peace, whose mind is stayed on You, because he trusts in You." The key is trust. The more we trust God, the more we allow His peace to reign in our hearts. It doesn't mean our circumstances will suddenly become easy, but it does mean that we'll have the strength to stand firm and walk forward, even when the path is difficult. It means trusting God's plan, even when we don't understand God's plan.

CHAPTER 12: THE SHOES OF THE GOSPEL OF PEACE

Reflection Questions:

1. Have you ever noticed that you're calm and peaceful in situations that would have torn you up before your salvation? Have your loved ones noticed this change in you as well?
2. Do you pray before and during sharing the Gospel to others? For example, praying for opportunities to share the Gospel, and for boldness and the words to point people to Christ?
3. How do you overcome fears or shyness about evangelizing to others?
4. How does your peace bear witness to the saving power of God?

Chapter 13: Unresolved Anger and Spiritual Warfare

"Be angry, and yet do not sin; do not let the sun go down on your anger, and do not give the devil an opportunity." Ephesians 4:26-27

We all get angry at times, yet *how* we process that anger is the question. When we allow anger to linger, and especially when we go to bed angry, it's like leaving the porch light on for the devil and his demons. Satan thrives on confusion, fear, and division. When we hang onto anger, bitterness and unforgiveness, we unknowingly give the enemy a foothold to stir up spiritual warfare.

There are also different types of anger. "Righteous indignation" is the kind of anger that stirs up when we see something that breaks God's heart, such as child abuse or Christian persecution. Romans 12:9 tells us to "Abhor what is evil" and Psalm 7:11 says that God is angry with the wicked every day.

Righteous anger differs from the anger we feel when someone cuts us off in traffic or when we're frustrated over a small offense. Righteous anger is the fire that rises up when we witness injustice, when God's holiness is disrespected, or when people are hurt in ways that go against His heart. It's the kind of anger that makes us stand up and say, "This is not right. This doesn't align with God's truth."

CHAPTER 13: UNRESOLVED ANGER AND SPIRITUAL WARFARE

Think about Jesus in John 2:15 when He was angry because because the money changers had turned His Father's house into a marketplace. The temple, a sacred place of worship, was being misused. Righteous anger is feeling God's heart break for what is broken in the world and wanting to do something about it.

Yet even righteous anger needs to be handled carefully. We can be furious about injustice, yet we mustn't allow that anger to lead us into bitterness or destructive actions. In everything we do, we must glorify God. It's about standing for what's right, speaking truth, but doing it in love, not out of vengeance.

In the end, righteous anger should propel us into action that reflects God's will such as fighting for justice, speaking for those who can't, and seeking reconciliation in a broken world. It's about fighting with a heart of love, compassion, and humility, and never letting that anger consume us, but always pointing people to the Gospel.

We also need to ascertain and pray whether the anger we're feeling is righteous. The Christian pastor and author Warren Wiersbe said, "Sometimes what we call 'righteous indignation' is only unrighteous temper masquerading in religious garments. Jesus equated anger with murder (Matthew 5:21-26), and Paul warns us that anger can hinder our praying (1 Timothy 2:8)."

The bottom line is to turn to God whenever you're angry. Don't allow a smoldering irritation to grow into bitterness, resentment, or rage. At the first hint of irritation, pray for God's wisdom and help. And most of all, don't go to sleep angry. Give the situation to God and trust that He will guide you.

Reflection Questions:

1. Is there unresolved anger in my life? Have I prayed for God to guide me in this area? Am I following God's wisdom and seeking

to glorify Him in this situation?
2. How can I handle my anger in a way that honors God and resolves it before it takes root in my heart?
3. What are some ways to deal with any anger I have while I'm falling asleep?
4. Have I prayed for my enemies, as Jesus commanded us to do?

Chapter 14: Jesus' Victory and Spiritual Warfare

When Jesus cried out, "It is finished" on the cross, He was declaring the victory of God's plan of redemption. Those who believe in Jesus' life, death, and resurrection and who put their trust in Him are forgiven, their relationship with God restored, and their soul is saved from the wrath for the sins we've all committed. Jesus' sacrifice on our behalf defeated death and the devil.

So, why do we Christians still endure spiritual warfare? Why are demons allowed to harass Christians? After all, we know that the devil was defeated on the cross and that the devil is on our sovereign God's short leash (Job 1-2). We also know that God created hell for the devil and his fallen angels (Matthew 25:41).

The devil is a defeated foe, yet he's allowed to roam the earth until Jesus' return. So, while we await Jesus' second coming, God has equipped up with His Word to resist the enemy and deal with spiritual warfare.

As I mentioned in the introduction to this book, I previously tried self-help methods to combat spiritual warfare such as deliverance ministries and books of prayers which supposedly routed out demons. These methods only offered temporary relief, followed by increased spiritual warfare. Finally when I chose to trust and follow God's instructions in the Bible, I found lasting relief from spiritual warfare. The Bible is sufficient!

Let me explain it like this: imagine a war has ended, and the enemy has been defeated. But, even though the outcome is certain, the enemy is still trying to wreak havoc until the final surrender. That's what we're living through right now. Satan knows he's defeated and his time on earth is coming to an end, but he's still fighting, and we're caught in the tension between the "already" and the "not yet."

Colossians 2:15 says, "Having disarmed principalities and powers, He made a public spectacle of them, triumphing over them in it." Jesus disarmed the enemy. He stripped away the power that the devil had over us such as sin, shame, fear, death. That was defeated at the cross. But we still live in a broken world where the effects of sin linger, where the enemy tries to trip us up, and where we continue to wrestle with temptation and spiritual opposition. The enemy is on a leash, and his days are numbered. But until Jesus returns, we live in the "in-between" which is the space between Christ's victory and the final judgment.

I know it can be frustrating at times. You may think, "If the victory is won, then why am I still struggling? Why is the enemy still attacking?" I've asked those same questions, and the Bible gives us answers. The weight of spiritual warfare can be overwhelming, and it can feel like we're constantly fighting an unseen enemy.

The Bible tells us that the devil runs this world (2 Corinthians 4:4), and that's why God consistently warns us to not conform to the world. We must beware of worldly influences such as materialism and carnality. Satan directs those who've rejected the Gospel. We look forward to the new heaven where there will be no more sin and God will wipe every tear from our eyes (Revelation 21:4).

Spiritual warfare can come from other people who are being influenced by the devil. The devil is the father of unsaved people (John 8:44) who are motivated by greed and sinful desires. This is why the Bible exhorts us to not be unequally yoked, because unsaved people

CHAPTER 14: JESUS' VICTORY AND SPIRITUAL WARFARE

can influence us in sinful ways. 2 Corinthians 6:14 says, "Do not be unequally yoked together with unbelievers. For what fellowship has righteousness with lawlessness? And what communion has light with darkness?" It's encouraging to remember that we are *in* the world, but we are not *of* the world (John 17:14-16). Once we are saved, this world is a temporary weigh station on our way to our permanent home in Heaven with Jesus and other believers.

Jesus has already defeated the enemy. The devil's head was crushed at the cross, and there's nothing he can do to change that (Genesis 3:15). Every attack, every lie, every attempt to steal your joy or peace is nothing more than a last-ditch swan song attempt by a defeated enemy.

Yes, we still deal with the enemy, but we also have the hope of Christ's return. In 1 Peter 5:8-9, Peter warns us to "Be sober-minded; be alert. Your adversary the devil is prowling around like a roaring lion, looking for anyone he can devour. Resist him, firm in the faith, knowing that the same kind of sufferings are being experienced by your brotherhood throughout the world." This is a reminder that the struggle is real, and we must be vigilant, but it's also an encouragement: we're not alone in this fight. And the struggle isn't forever. We are on the winning side.

The tension we feel, the frustration of living in a world still affected by sin, the emotional and spiritual warfare we face, the relentless attacks of the enemy—will all come to an end one day. Jesus is coming back, and when He does, He will put an end to all of it. Revelation 20:10 tells us, "And the devil who had deceived them was thrown into the lake of fire and sulfur where the beast and the false prophet were, and they will be tormented day and night forever and ever." That's the final, ultimate victory. In the new heaven, there will be no more tears, no more sin, and no more spiritual warfare. Praise God!

The victory is ours in Christ, but we still have a role to play. The enemy may try to discourage us, but we can stand in the knowledge that Jesus has already won. The cross is the proof, and the resurrection is the guarantee that the final victory is secure.

This means that when we face spiritual battles, we don't need to panic or give in to fear. We can stand firm, not in our own strength, but in the strength of the One who has already defeated the enemy. Ephesians 6:10-11 says, "Be strengthened by the Lord and by His vast strength. Put on the full Armor of God so that you can stand against the schemes of the devil." The Armor of God is our protection, our assurance that we're equipped to face the enemy's attacks while resting in the victory of Christ.

Reflection Questions:

1. How do you deal with frustration about ongoing spiritual battles?
2. Have any worldly desires interfered with your desire to keep your eyes upon Jesus?
3. Have you been unequally yoked with unbelievers at work, school, or at home? Have they influenced you, or were you able to stay strong in Christ and perhaps share the Gospel with them?
4. How do you deal with fears about spiritual warfare, so that you're reassured of Christ's victory and the temporariness of our battles here on earth?

Chapter 15: Sin's Role in Spiritual Warfare

As Christians, we face three sources of temptation: our flesh, the world, and the devil. Our fleshly desires are the body's cravings for sin such as drunkenness, gluttony, or sexual sin. This is described as someone "whose god is their belly" in Philippians 3:19. Fortunately, one of the fruits of the Spirit is self-control to deal with these cravings. We also need to turn to God for strength to combat these temptations.

Worldly influences can include envy or coveting what someone else owns or trying to seek admiration and self-glory instead of doing everything for the glory of God. Worldly music and movies can also offer sinful influences to professing Christians if they're not alert and aware.

We're warning about the devil's influences throughout this book and learning what the Bible teaches us about preparation and protection against this spiritual warfare. One of the biggest factors that guards us from spiritual warfare is avoiding falling into unrepentant sin. That's because sin is a major factor in spiritual warfare.

As we know, even after we come to Christ, sinful temptations don't just disappear. And when we don't deal with them, or when we ignore or minimize them, we can give the enemy a foothold in our lives. It's like leaving a door open and inviting him in.

When we repent, He is faithful to forgive us. But there's a difference between knowing Jesus forgives and walking in ongoing unrepentant sin. And that difference can have serious spiritual consequences.

The devil is so evil that he tries to capitalize upon our weaknesses. When we live in sin, especially sin we've allowed to stay hidden, we give him a foothold. He uses guilt, shame, and condemnation to weigh us down. The longer we hold onto sin, the more we become susceptible to spiritual oppression.

The Bible says that when we are hypocrites we have a "seared conscience" (1 Timothy 4:2) that can no longer sense the Holy Spirit's warnings about the spiritual danger that we're in. And this is where spiritual warfare kicks in. When we continue to sin, we open ourselves to the enemy's schemes, lies, accusations, and attempts to make us feel unworthy and defeated. At that point our mind and conscience become defiled (Titus 1:15). There's a likelihood in situations that go this far, that the person wasn't saved in the first place.

This isn't just about one type of sin. Maybe for you, it's pride, lust, gossip, or anger. Maybe it's something no one else can see. The Bible says, "Whoever conceals their sins does not prosper, but the one who confesses and renounces them finds mercy" (Proverbs 28:13). When we hide sin, it grows in the darkness. And of course it's impossible to hide sin from our all-knowing God. When we bring sin to His light through repentance, we are forgiven. We need to repent daily, because we sin daily either in our thoughts or in our actions.

Repentance is more than saying, "I'm sorry" or feeling guilty for what we've done. Repentance is a heartfelt turning away from sin and turning toward God. It's realizing that we've done something wrong and, in godly sorrow, we seek to make it right. 2 Corinthians 7:10 says, "For godly grief produces a repentance that leads to salvation without regret, but worldly grief produces death." *Godly grief (also known as godly sorrow)* means that your heart is broken to think that you rebelled against our holy God Whom you love and want to please. In contrast, *worldly grief (also known as worldly sorrow)* is feeling bad about getting caught or about the consequences of sin.

Repenting and praying for God to give you the strength to resist temptation and to take away your craving for the sin, will strengthen your relationship with God. "Draw near to God, and He will draw near to you. Cleanse your hands, you sinners; and purify your hearts, you double-minded" (James 4:8) emphasizes the importance of seeking a closer relationship with God and to pray for spiritual purification.

In 1 John 1:9 we're reminded, "If we confess our sins, he is faithful and just to forgive us our sins and to cleanse us from all unrighteousness." God's forgiveness is immediate and complete. It's not about earning forgiveness or doing penance; it's about receiving His grace with a repentant heart. And that's where true freedom begins.

Sin doesn't just affect our relationship with God. It affects our relationship with ourselves and other people. When we allow unconfessed sin to remain, we know deep down that we're messing up and that fills us with guilt, sorrow, and even self-hatred. The devil takes advantage of these vulnerabilities and pounces upon us with spiritual warfare in an effort to steer us further from God. Fortunately, when we bring our sins to God in genuine repentance, He washes us clean and restores us.

Jesus died to take the punishment that we all deserve for our sins. His work on the cross is finished and we are forgiven.

Reflection Questions:

1. Is there anything you're currently doing that you know is sinful? Have you turned to God for repentance and the strength to stop the sinful actions?
2. Can you think of a time in your life when you realized you were sinning, and so you repented? How did that affect you, before and after repentance?

3. How can you help a friend who's involved with unrepentant sin?
4. Sometimes the devil tries to make us feel ashamed about our past sins that we've repented for and have turned away from. How can we deal with these lies from the enemy that try to rob our joy?

Chapter 16: Bad Decisions and Spiritual Warfare

Sometimes, what seems like spiritual warfare is actually a consequence of sin or poor choices that we've made. Have you ever impulsively made a decision, only to later regret leaping before you looked?

The consequences of past sin are painful. Yes, your sins are forgiven the moment that you repent and put your trust in Jesus as your Lord and Savior. However, forgiven sins don't erase the earthly price we must pay for our sins. Think about the pain that Solomon and Bathsheba endured in losing their first-born child after their sinful affair.

Poor decisions can be an effect of not trusting the Lord. Perhaps you believe that you must do everything yourself. Or maybe you have issues with trusting others (including God!) to help you. Perhaps you believe that you need to control situations yourself, instead of following God's lead. Usually, these situations are from not knowing God and can be remedied by studying the Bible daily to learn about His attributes, character, and promises. It's also helpful to review the ways that God has helped you (especially salvation!) over the years.

So, if you made poor choices about your finances, you may suffer financially today. If you were injured while engaging in a risky activity, your health may suffer today. If you betrayed your spouse, your marriage may suffer today. That's not spiritual warfare. That's a consequence of making unwise decisions. Of course, the devil will try to take advantage of any vulnerabilities.

This is not about beating yourself up with guilt, shame or regret over poor decisions. Learning from our mistakes is a positive result, but berating ourselves is not helpful. Sometimes there's a combined effect of spiritual warfare and bad decisions, because the demons may have brought the temptations that led to those sinful choices.

The Bible is filled with stories of those who sinned, yet God still used them in mighty ways. After all, only Jesus is sinless. When we consider how God used Saul/Paul after he persecuted Christians, then we won't believe the devil's lies about being disqualified because of our past sins.

Poor choices lead to their own set of consequences. And while spiritual warfare can feel like you're being attacked, poor decisions are more like self-inflicted wounds from reaping the consequences of actions that didn't align with God's Word.

For example, if you've been dishonest in your relationships, you might face the natural consequences of broken trust or strained connections. If you've ignored God's calling on your life or made decisions without His guidance, you might experience a lack of peace or direction. If you've neglected your health or finances, you might struggle with the consequences of not managing them well. These consequences can feel heavy and overwhelming, just like spiritual attacks, but they're not coming from the enemy directly. They're the natural outcomes of decisions we've made.

To make matters worse, the enemy may leap upon these consequences of prior sins. The devil will accuse you until you're so filled with guilt and shame that you hesitate in sharing the Gospel with others.

The important thing here is recognizing your role in these struggles. Taking responsibility for past sins is a mature way to learn and grow, so you won't repeat the same poor choices. By taking responsibility, you're more apt to be careful in the future. Taking responsibility is a

CHAPTER 16: BAD DECISIONS AND SPIRITUAL WARFARE

far better approach than beating yourself up with guilt and shame – especially since the devil may take advantage of you when you're down. That's when problems seem to pour in at the same time.

So, take responsibility for your past sins. Repent to God for these sins, and pray for Him to help you to learn, grow, and not repeat these sins. Apologize to the people you may have hurt and do your best to make amends. I love this prayer from Psalm 139:23-24: "Search me, O God, and know my heart; Try me, and know my anxieties; And see if there is any wicked way in me, And lead me in the way everlasting."

The consequences of past sins and poor decisions can overlap with spiritual warfare, so there's no clear cut distinctions. The results are painful and often frightening. So, if you're enduring a season of struggle with these consequences, please don't feel like it's a penalty for your sins that you have to endure alone. God is still with you if you've repented and trust in Jesus. Micah 7:18-19 says that God "does not retain His anger forever, because He delights in mercy. He will again have compassion on us, and will subdue our iniquities."

Remember to ask God for wisdom as you navigate through these consequences. James 1:5 reminds us, "If any of you lacks wisdom, let him ask of God, who gives to all liberally and without reproach, and it will be given to him." God is not in the business of leaving you in confusion. When in doubt, pray and ask God for wisdom. He will guide you primarily through your Bible study, to help you navigate this trial. Don't underestimate the power of asking Him for clarity in these situations.

It's also a good idea to seek wise counsel. Proverbs 11:14 says, "Where there is no guidance, a people falls, but in an abundance of counselors there is safety." If you're unsure how to manage the consequences of your past sins and poor decisions, seek wise and godly counsel from someone you trust even if it's embarrassing to admit what you did in the past. Everyone is a sinner, and a mature Christian will understand especially if there's fruit of repentance. Sometimes it can be hard to see the truth about our own decisions when we're too close to the situation. A godly friend, mentor, Bible study teacher, or pastor can help you see things clearly and offer perspective.

Whether your trials are from spiritual warfare or the consequences of poor decisions, God has a plan to help you to endure. If you're dealing with spiritual attacks, remember to put on the Armor of God, submit to God and resist the devil. And if the trials you're currently enduring are the result of poor decisions, confess them to God. 1 John 1:9 reassures us: "If we confess our sins, He is faithful and just to forgive us our sins and to cleanse us from all unrighteousness."

Reflection Questions:

1. How do you deal with shame or regret about your past mistakes?
2. In what ways are you learning to trust God and not trying to control everything yourself?
3. Can you think of a time when the devil attacked you with accusations that caused you to doubt yourself? How did you overcome this experience?
4. Do you think some people incorrectly blame all their problems on demons, when in reality some problems occur because of our own mistakes?

Remember sister, God is with you in all things - whether it's a spiritual battle or a tough season of learning from your mistakes. He'll guide you, heal you, and help you walk through it with strength. Keep your eyes on Him.

Chapter 17: The Truth about Deliverance Ministries

When I was first saved and suffering from spiritual warfare for the first time that I was aware of, I didn't know what to do. I hadn't read much of the Bible yet, and I didn't know any mature Christians to guide me.

So, I searched on the Internet for "spiritual warfare" and found advertisements from "deliverance ministries" who guaranteed they could cast out demons and curses. I spent a lot of time and money chasing after peace with these deliverance ministries and reading deliverance ministry books. They promised to give me special prayers that would rout out demons. Yet, the results were only fleeting temporary moments of peace, followed by increased spiritual warfare.

Finally, when I studied the Bible's instructions about dealing with spiritual warfare, I found relief and peace. God has equipped us in His Word on how to deal with the inevitable attacks from the enemy.

So, as your sister in Christ who has:

- been-there-done-that with deliverance ministries (including the new age version of deliverance called "depossession" or "spirit releasement therapy")
- interviewed other sisters who've been hurt by deliverance ministries

- interviewed a former deliverance minister who has since repented and now warns others about the perils of deliverance ministries
- compared what the deliverance ministries are saying, to what the Bible says,

please know that I'm cautioning you because I care about you. Some will get upset by my words, because deliverance ministries are a huge profitable industry and they don't like their business model threatened.

But here's the Biblical truth: there's not a single story in the Bible where a saved person is possessed by a demon. *One hundred percent of the people from whom Jesus and the apostles cast out demons, were unsaved people.* And while there are many false deliverance ministries out there trying to convince us that Christians can be possessed, we have to hold tightly to the truth of God's Word. Any demonstrations of exorcisms from deliverance ministries are either from their theatrics, or because they're working with unsaved people or false converts (those who claim to be a Christian but actually aren't).

The Bible teaches that saved Christians can be *oppressed* (harassed by demons that are outside of their body), but not *possessed* (because the indwelling Holy Spirit within Christians won't allow demons to reside with Him). The spiritual warfare we're discussing in this book is oppression.

In the Bible, we see Jesus and the apostles casting demons out of unsaved people who weren't believers until *after* the demons were cast out of them. They were living in darkness, without the protection of the Holy Spirit. Demons had a hold on them, and they needed to be set free.

Let's pause for a moment. The idea that a Christian can be possessed is simply not supported by Scripture. Why? Because the Bible makes it clear that the moment we place our faith in Jesus Christ, we're sealed with the Holy Spirit (Ephesians 1:13-14). The Spirit of God takes

CHAPTER 17: THE TRUTH ABOUT DELIVERANCE MINISTRIES

residence in us, and He's not going to share that space with demons. It's not about us being perfect or without struggle; it's about the fact that the Holy Spirit dwells within us, and nothing can separate us from God's love (Romans 8:38-39).

If you're a Christian, your body is a temple of the Holy Spirit (1 Corinthians 6:19-20). God Himself chooses to dwell in you. Now, would He allow a demon to possess the very temple He calls His own? No, He wouldn't. This truth should bring you peace, not fear.

There are ministries and teachers out there who claim that Christians can be possessed by demons. They say things like, "You need deliverance because the enemy is still inside of you because of your past dealings with the occult," or "You're not truly free unless you've been exorcised." These ideas sound spiritual and convincing, but they don't line up with what we see in the Bible.

Let's look at the ministry of Jesus and the apostles. Every single demon Jesus cast out was from an *unsaved* person. Think about it: the man with the legion of demons (Mark 5:1-20), the woman with the spirit of divination (Acts 16:16-18), the demon-possessed boy (Mark 9:14-29) - none of these people were saved. And it's important to note that Jesus never, ever cast a demon out of a believer. The apostles followed Jesus' example. They cast out demons, but again, these were people who didn't know Christ.

So, why do these false ministries exist? Unfortunately, there are some who prey upon believers' fear of spiritual warfare and the unknown. They create a narrative where if you're struggling with sin or if you're facing hardship, it must be because you've got demons living inside of you. And they offer "deliverance" as the solution. Perhaps these "deliverance ministers" are well-meaning and themselves deceived. Nonetheless, they don't offer biblical services.

Deliverance ministries are big lucrative businesses, and they claim their critics have a "religious spirit" (a term that doesn't exist in the

Bible). They also accuse their critics of blaspheming the Holy Spirit, yet that term applies exclusively to people who reject the Gospel.

Just because you face struggles doesn't mean you're possessed. Struggles come from many sources: spiritual oppression, our own weaknesses, or the consequences of living in a broken world. But none of those struggles automatically mean a demon is controlling you from the inside. Sometimes, it's the enemy's oppression trying to disrupt your peace or pull you away from God's purpose for your life. Other times as we've seen in this book, it's the consequences of our past sins and poor decisions.

What's even more dangerous is that these false deliverance teachings can cause you to doubt your salvation. If you're a Christian, the Holy Spirit lives in you. You're sealed, protected, and secure in Christ. But false deliverance ministries can make you feel like you're incomplete, like you're missing something, or that you need to do something extra to be truly free. To them, Jesus' finished work on the cross is not enough. Some deliverance ministries insist that their customers return for "maintenance" to cast out demons on a regular basis. That is a lie. The work Jesus did on the cross was complete.

You don't need to be "re-delivered" from demons because Jesus already defeated them for you. The moment you were saved, the demons were cast out of you and the Holy Spirit indwelled you.

Deliverance ministries argue that Jesus gave us authority to cast out demons. Yet, that's not the issue at all. This is not about "authority." It's about the fact that Christians can't be possessed, and anyone who says otherwise is either ignorant about the Bible or is a con-artist. Deliverance ministries conduct highly theatrical "deliverances" from people who claim to be Christians. Their clients shudder, drool, vomit, and fall on the floor as the demons are supposedly cast out of them. Yet it's all hypnotic theatrics. These deliverance ministries may claim to be free of charge, but most have high-pressure sales techniques to get

CHAPTER 17: THE TRUTH ABOUT DELIVERANCE MINISTRIES

donations or sell books, DVD's, maintenance appointments, seminars, and so forth. It's best to avoid these deliverance ministries.

Now, let's be clear: spiritual oppression is real. The enemy can attack us, and we'll face spiritual warfare. You might feel like you're being weighed down with fear, anxiety, temptation, or even confusion. But that is oppression, not possession. Oppression is when the enemy pressures us or tries to influence us from the outside. Possession is when he takes control from the inside. And as a believer, the enemy has no ability to possess you.

You might be wondering, "What about my struggles with sin and temptation?" That's real, too. When we give in to sin, we may become more vulnerable to spiritual attack, but that's not the same as being demon-possessed. The key is to repent and turn back to God (1 John 1:9). When we do, the enemy has to flee. We may still face temptation and struggle, but we're not under the enemy's control.

Here's the bottom line: If you're a born-again Christian, you're not possessed by demons. The moment you were saved, Jesus delivered you from any demons that may have possessed you before your salvation. His deliverance is complete, and you don't need any further deliverance because the Second Person of the Holy Trinity resides inside of you.

You may face spiritual warfare, oppression, and struggle, but you're sealed by the Holy Spirit, and your identity in Christ is secure. Remember that Jesus on the cross won the victory over sin, death and the devil. The enemy has been defeated, and you don't need to be afraid. Instead, walk in the freedom that Jesus gives you. If you're struggling, turn to Him, seek His strength, and know that you have everything you need in Him.

Reflection Questions:

1. Have you or someone you know tried a deliverance ministry? How

did it go?
2. How does it feel to know that all Christians are sealed by the indwelling Holy Spirit?
3. What have you learned so far about the Armor of God?
4. When you face spiritual warfare, what are some ways that you can have the strength to resist the devil's schemes and temptations?

Chapter 18: Items in Your Home and Spiritual Warfare

If there are new age or occult items in your home, they could be another cause of increased spiritual warfare. Now, the items themselves aren't possessed. It's the fact that they're in your home that's the problem.

New Age, witchcraft, and sorcery are clearly condemned in the Old Testament and the New Testament of the Bible. They're grievous sins for which our Lord and Savior Jesus died. Those who practice sorcery won't be allowed into the new heaven but will be cast into the lake of fire for eternal torment (Revelation 21:8, 22:15). Sorcery is also linked to idolatry (praying to demons or statues) and witchcraft (trying to conjure something to happen). These are amongst the sins for which Jesus died on the cross, and we don't want to have anything to do with them.

Having new age or occultic items in your home leads to increased spiritual warfare, because having these items is a sin. It's rebellion against our holy God Who saved us out of darkness. Yes, we have Christian liberty and freedom to do what is not explicitly called a sin in the Bible. If God calls something a sin, then there's no liberty or freedom to do it.

Divination, astrology, tarot, Wicca, witchcraft, mediumship, paganism and idolatry are amongst the sins that we must avoid. So, we can't have items related to these topics in our home. We must discard or burn these items, to get them out of circulation so the items don't deceive other people. For that reason, we shouldn't donate or sell the items.

The Bible is clear that we are to flee from evil and avoid any connection with condemned practices (Deuteronomy 18:9-14; Ephesian 5:11). We're also told not to do anything that could cause someone else to stumble into deception. And if a friend saw these items in your home, she may assume that it's okay for Christians to have new age or occultic items when it's not.

Acts 19:18-19 shows a powerful example of repentant Christians burning their sorcery books and occultic items. The value of the items they burned was 50,000 pieces of silver. Please keep this in mind if you're reluctant to discard your new age items because they were expensive. The cost of keeping them is even higher in terms of spiritual warfare, rebelliously sinning, and increasing temptation to sin by having the items in your home. When we hold onto these items for whatever reason, we're unknowingly inviting oppression. The enemy works in subtle ways through whatever crack he can find. And these objects, even if we don't actively use them, can be that crack.

You may feel a hesitation to get rid of these things. I understand that. It's hard to part with something that's tied to your past or even your identity. But imagine the peace that will come when you remove anything that doesn't glorify God.

When you actively clear your home of these items, you're taking a stand against the enemy. We need to glorify God in everything we do. New age and occultic items glorify the devil, or false portrayals of God (such as calling God "the universe) and they glorify the self with sinful pride. New age and occultic items don't glorify God.

If you're wondering, "What should I do with these things?" here's the answer: Don't just hide them away. Don't try to hold onto them for "safekeeping." Get rid of them. You don't need to hold onto anything from your past that has a hold upon you. If you think of these occultic

CHAPTER 18: ITEMS IN YOUR HOME AND SPIRITUAL WARFARE

new age items fondly like old friends, that's a giant red flag. Throw them out, burn them safely, or dispose of them in a way that is permanent, so the items don't cause others to stumble into deception.

Sister remember: your home is a reflection of your heart. Don't let anything take root there that doesn't honor God.

Reflection Questions:

1. Are there any items in your home that might be linked to the occult or new age practices that you need to dispose?
2. What are some items you can add to your home that glorify God?
3. How can you overcome any hesitation you may have about disposing of new age or occultic items?
4. Does your spouse or roommate have any new age or occultic items in the home you share? How can you discuss this important topic with them? (This is something also to pray for God's wisdom about).

Chapter 19: Prayer and Spiritual Warfare

In the midst of spiritual battles, we must remember to pray for God's protection, provision, strength, and boldness. Yet, we also need to beware of false teachings that offer to sell us formulaic prayers that are "guaranteed to rout out demons."

In times of spiritual battle, we may be tempted to look for a quick fix such as a book of formulaic prayer that promises to drive out evil or shield us from harm. But let us be reminded that no specific prayer, no matter how perfectly crafted or recited, guarantees a victory over evil on its own. There's no magic incantation, no "one-size-fits-all" prayer that will automatically silence the forces of darkness. We can't hand God a scripted prayer and expect Him to obey. God is God, and He can't be manipulated or coerced. God's plans and timing are perfect, and we need to trust in His ways.

The heart of spiritual warfare is not our ability to say the right things, but our willingness to humble ourselves before God and seek His will. It's about our heart's attitude toward Him and our complete dependence on His power. As the Lord's Prayer instructs us, we should earnestly pray, "Deliver us from evil" (Matthew 6:13). This simple but profound petition from our Lord Jesus reminds us that we can't fight spiritual battle alone. We need God's intervention to overcome the forces of evil and deliver us from the snares of the enemy.

When we pray for deliverance from evil, it's essential that we

CHAPTER 19: PRAYER AND SPIRITUAL WARFARE

understand what we're asking. Jesus delivered any indwelling demons out of us the moment that we repented for our sins and put our trust in Him. The moment we were saved, the demons were cast out of us through Jesus' shed blood on the cross.

At that moment of salvation, the Holy Spirit indwelled us and sealed us so that we couldn't be possessed by evil. Only unsaved people and false converts (who don't have the Holy Spirit within them) can be possessed. Those who are saved Christians can be oppressed by demons outside of them harassing them. But Christians will never have demons inside of them.

That means that our prayer, "Deliver us from evil" is asking God to protect us from spiritual warfare and oppression. Every day we face temptations, trials, and challenges that require us to seek God's help. Our prayers should reflect an honest and authentic desire to trust Him in the midst of these struggles. Like the Psalmist, we need to pour out our heart transparently to God and tell Him everything we're feeling and thinking. He already knows this anyway. As we pray, it's important to sincerely praise God for the blessings that we have, especially for our salvation.

In prayer, we need to ask for His protection, guidance, and grace to stand firm in our faith. Prayer isn't about coercing God to act on our terms. Prayer is about changing ourselves, and about aligning ourselves with His will and submitting to His authority.

Spiritual warfare calls us to submit to God and resist the devil (James 4:7). *Submitting to God* means obeying His 10 commandments, including loving God and loving our neighbors. Jesus is the Lord of the Sabbath Who is our rest (Matthew 12:8), so our fulfillment of the 4th commandment is by abiding in Christ. In the Bible, "loving God" also means trusting and obeying Him. Jesus said, "If you love me, keep my commandments" (John 14:15). When we say that Jesus is our Lord and our King, we demonstrate our sincerity through our actions, reverence, worship, and obedience.

Resisting the devil means making choices to remove ourselves from sinful temptations. If you have a history of drunkenness, for example, stay away from bars and pubs. If you have a history of adultery, stay away from pornography and flirtatious people. If you have a history of gluttony, be careful what snacks you store in your home. If you have a history with new age deception, avoid crystal shops and mind-body-spirit festivals. Resisting the devil means thinking around the corner and removing yourself from potentially spiritually dangerous situations.

The real battle of spiritual warfare often occurs within our own hearts. The enemy's attacks may manifest externally in our circumstances or relationships, but they often stem from internal struggles with sin, fear, and doubt. Our prayers must therefore be honest and heartfelt, acknowledging our own weaknesses and asking God to help us submit to His authority. We must pray for strength to resist the temptation to take matters into our own hands, to act out of fear or pride, and to instead humbly yield to God's will.

As Psalm 51:17 says, "The sacrifices of God are a broken spirit, A broken and a contrite heart – These, O God, You will not despise." This verse means that God wants us to have humble and repentant hearts, and that He is compassionate toward those who approach Him with sincerity and humility.

In praying for deliverance, we must recognize that the battle for our hearts is just as crucial as the battle for our circumstances. We're called to submit to God's will and resist the devil, knowing that only through submission to God's authority can we truly experience victory. The Bible teaches us in James 4:7, "Submit yourselves, then, to God. Resist the devil, and he will flee from you." Submission is not a sign of weakness, but an act of strength - acknowledging that God is the ultimate authority in our lives and that we are fully dependent on His

CHAPTER 19: PRAYER AND SPIRITUAL WARFARE

power to fight the enemy.

There's no specific set of words in prayers that will guarantee that God will bend to your will. The very thought of that is the opposite of a humble submissive heart. We need to avoid books that teach these formulaic prayers. Spiritual warfare is about *faith* in God's power, not about do-it-yourself recitations of specific prayers or chants.

Those books are man-centered approaches to life, in attempts to manipulate God. Trust in the Lord with all of your heart (Proverbs 3:5) means trusting that He hears your sincere prayers and answers them according to His will, His timing, and His way. In 2 Corinthians 1:9, Paul explains that all of the hardships that he endured was to help Paul to lean upon God and not upon his own strength.

Instead of looking for magic prayer formulas, we should approach God with a humble and open heart, acknowledging our need for His help. As we face the battles of life, we must remember that it's not our own power that will bring victory, but God's power. It's about trusting in God's sovereignty and submitting to His will that He clearly outlines in the Bible. As we pray, we invite Him into our battles, knowing that He is faithful and able to deliver us from evil. In the midst of the battle, may our prayer always be: "Deliver us from evil," and may we find the strength to submit to God's will, knowing that in He is already victorious.

Reflection Questions:

1. Do you ever feel shy about admitting your vulnerable thoughts and feelings to God? Does it help to remember that God already knows what you think and feel, and that He still cares for you?
2. Have you ever fallen for the scheme of "formula prayer books" that promise guaranteed results? What was that like for you?
3. What helps you to remember to pray for God's help, instead of

trying to manage and control situations on your own?
4. Which prayers have been answered in ways that differed from your expectations? Aren't you glad that God answered your prayers in His way?

Chapter 20: When God Tests Us

Sometimes we go through seasons of struggle where it seems like it's one battle after another. For example, financial strain, relationship challenges, health concerns, or grief over losses. When everything seems to hit you at once, it's overwhelming and seems like the demons have been unleashed upon you. Yet, the Bible reminds us that not every difficult situation in our lives is a direct attack from the enemy.

The hard things we face aren't always about the enemy trying to drag us down. They can be part of God's loving process of refining and growing us. God tests and prunes those whom He loves.

It's important to understand the difference. When we're facing spiritual warfare, we're often directly confronting the enemy's schemes, his lies, or his temptations. Spiritual warfare is about resisting the evil one and standing firm against his attacks. But there are moments when God allows us to face trials as a test or a way to build our faith or endurance. This isn't spiritual warfare; it's God's tool for growth.

1. The Purpose of God's Tests

God's tests help to refine us, to make us more like Christ. In James 1:2-4, we're told, "Consider it pure joy, my brothers and sisters, whenever you face trials of many kinds, because you know that the testing of your faith produces perseverance. Let perseverance finish its work so that you may be mature and complete, not lacking anything."

Now, you're probably thinking: *Joy in trials?* Really? But here's the thing: God uses trials to develop something in us that wouldn't grow otherwise. They're not meant to destroy us; they're meant to refine us, just like gold in a fire. It's painful, yes, but the result is growth.

Perhaps you can recall a time when you went through testing of your faith. You may have been shaken and frightened, yet you still had faith in God helping you. And when He did help you, your faith grew stronger as a result.

These tests don't mean you're doing something wrong; they mean that God is allowing you to stretch your faith and learn to depend on Him more deeply.

2. Testing Vs Temptation

Sometimes we get confused between testing and temptation. Testing comes from God, and it's meant to strengthen and refine us. Temptation, on the other hand, comes from the enemy and seeks to lead us away from God's will. Let's break this down a little.

In James 1:13, it says, "When tempted, no one should say, 'God is tempting me.' For God cannot be tempted by evil, nor does he tempt anyone." Temptation is always a ploy by the enemy to get us to sin, to go against God's plan. But testing, on the other hand, is part of God's loving process of sanctification.

When you're tested by God, He's not trying to trip you up or cause you to stumble. He's giving you an opportunity to trust Him more deeply. When you're tempted by the enemy, he's trying to pull you away from God's will and lead you into sin. God wants you to grow, and the devil wants you to fail. That's the difference.

3. Examples of God Testing His People

Throughout Scripture, we see God testing His people. Think about Abraham. God called him to sacrifice Isaac, his beloved son. That was a test. God knew what Abraham would do, but He wanted to give Abraham the chance to demonstrate his faith. Abraham passed the test, and God provided a ram in Isaac's place.

Then there's the story of Job whose life was turned upside down. His wealth, health, and family were all taken from him. But that trial wasn't an attack from the enemy - it was a test from God. God allowed Satan to test Job's faithfulness, but He never abandoned Job. And in the end, Job's faith was refined and strengthened.

God's tests in our lives may not always make sense in the moment, but we can be sure of one thing: He is with us in the trial, refining us, and preparing us for what's ahead.

4. How to Tell the Difference: Testing vs. Spiritual Warfare

You might be wondering, *'How do I know if I'm going through a test from God or an attack from the enemy?'* Here are some differences to notice:

• If you feel like your faith is being tested and refined, and you're being challenged to trust God more deeply, it's probably a test from God.

• If you feel like you're being led toward sin or tempted to doubt God's goodness, it's likely spiritual warfare.

Another key difference is that God's tests always lead to learning and growth. Even if it feels difficult or uncomfortable, His tests have a purpose: to mold and shape you to be more like Jesus. On the other hand, spiritual warfare is designed to distract, discourage, and destroy your faith.

5. The Benefit of Endurance in Trials

James goes on to tell us in James 1:12, "Blessed is the one who perseveres under trial because, having stood the test, that person will receive the crown of life that the Lord has promised to those who love him."

In the testing, there is blessing. There's growth, and there's reward. Persevering through a test builds endurance. And when you endure with faith, God is glorified, and you are strengthened.

6. What to Do When You're Being Tested

If you're in a season of testing, here are a few practical things to remember:

• **Ask God for wisdom**. James 1:5 tells us, "If any of you lacks wisdom, let him ask of God, who gives to all liberally and without reproach, and it will be given to him." God wants to guide you through the test and give you the wisdom to navigate it.

• **Persevere with joy**. Again, this doesn't mean the trial is easy or painless, yet joy comes from knowing that God is at work in you. He's using this situation to refine your faith.

• **Lean into God's strength**. You can't do it on your own. The tests you face will stretch you, but you don't have to face them alone. God will give you the strength to endure.

Sweet sister, if you're walking through a season of testing right now, don't lose heart. God is refining you, strengthening you, and drawing you closer to Himself. Trust that He has a purpose in every trial, even when you don't understand it. And remember: the enemy doesn't get the last word. He may try to use trials to pull you away from God, but God is using them to shape you into someone more like Christ.

Reflection Questions:

1. Can you think of a recent trial in your life that might have been God testing your faith? What is God teaching you through it?

2. What areas of your life have you felt tempted to doubt God's goodness? How can you combat those lies with truth?

3. How do you typically respond to tests or challenges in your life? Are there ways you can lean more into God's strength and wisdom in those moments?

4. What might it look like for you to embrace trials with joy, knowing they are refining you for God's purposes?

CHAPTER 20: WHEN GOD TESTS US

Sister, remember that tests aren't meant to harm you but to help you grow. God's tests bring transformation, not destruction. Keep trusting Him, even when the road feels tough.

Chapter 21: God's Pruning Process and Spiritual Warfare

Sometimes it feels like your life is being peeled away like an orange. A friend stops returning your texts. A job opportunity doesn't come through. The loan you applied for is declined. Is this spiritual warfare, or is God pruning away that which doesn't fit His plan for you?

Pruning is a word used often in the Bible to describe how God works in our lives. In John 15:2, Jesus says, "He cuts off every branch in me that bears no fruit, while every branch that does bear fruit he prunes so that it will be even more fruitful."

I've had moments where I've felt like God was cutting away parts of me that I thought were essential, such as people I'd grown attached to, or things that were comfortable and familiar. But as He pruned, I began to see the fruit of patience, love, and endurance grow in my life.

When God prunes us, it's not because He's angry with us or punishing us - it's because He loves us. He knows that for us to grow, some weights need to be removed. Whether it's a friendship, a habit, or even a mindset, pruning often feels like a loss. But when we look at it through the lens of His love, we realize that it's a necessary step toward becoming who He created us to be. And as painful as pruning can be, when we look back afterward, we can see God's loving fingerprint on His artistry. This helps us to trust God when pruning happens in the future.

CHAPTER 21: GOD'S PRUNING PROCESS AND SPIRITUAL WARFARE

Some people may mistakenly believe that the pruning process is spiritual warfare, because both are painful and frightening in the moment. Of course, the obvious difference is that pruning comes from God, while spiritual warfare originates with the devil.

Unlike pruning, which is a process of growth and refinement, spiritual warfare feels like an attack on your spirit. The Bible tells us that "our struggle is not against flesh and blood, but against the rulers, against the authorities, against the powers of this dark world" (Ephesians 6:12). The enemy will try to make you feel isolated, unlovable, rejected, and even defeated. The devil's entire agenda is to trick you into following him instead of Jesus, because the devil is trying to compete with God to win more souls.

I've found that one of the clearest indicators that I'm in a season of spiritual warfare is when the attacks come suddenly and relentlessly, often accompanied by fear or confusion. When I'm being pruned, I feel a certain peace in the process, even though it's painful. But when the enemy is attacking, there's a sense of retaliation, chaos and unrest that leaves me questioning everything around me. The lies from the enemy can feel like they come from all sides, and the heaviness of it all can be overwhelming.

In the midst of trials, it may not be apparent in the moment whether it's God's pruning or the devil's spiritual warfare. We often can't see the blessings of God removing toxic relationships and unhealthy situations from us, until after the fact.

So whatever trial you're enduring, it's important to pray for God's wisdom, strength, courage, and protection. It's equally important to trust God to see you through the situation. Sometimes God removes options, to steer us in a better direction. And always, God wants us to rely upon Him instead of ourselves.

God's pruning is not about defense; it's about growth. His pruning process brings clarity and removes distractions. The goal is to make you more fruitful in Him, like a branch that bears much fruit because it has been properly tended.

Both pruning and spiritual warfare are part of our spiritual journeys, and while they may seem similar in their challenges, they're entirely different in their purposes. One brings growth and refinement, the other brings resistance and discouragement. When you're in a season of pruning, remember that God's work is to beautify your soul, and He's right there with you in the discomfort. God is the vinedresser (John 15:1-2) and He knows the difference between cutting away the dead weight to make you more fruitful, and when the enemy is trying to tempt or deceive you. God is with you in all trials.

Reflection Questions:

1. Have you ever lost a friendship, only to later realize that the person wasn't a true friend after all? Do you believe God pruned that relationship? Did the process of pruning draw you closer to God and help you to grow as a Christian?
2. Have you ever been turned down for a job, only to get a better job later? Weren't you glad that you didn't get the first job?
3. When you think back upon these pruning processes, in what ways did they differ from the spiritual warfare you've experienced?
4. What has helped you to grow in your walk with Christ, and learn to trust Him?

Chapter 22: When God Disciplines Us

There are seasons in life when it feels like the weight of the world is crashing down on us, when we're pressed from every side. We can feel overwhelmed, defeated, and confused. As we've seen in the last few chapters, sometimes these trials are God steering us, and not from spiritual warfare.

In this chapter, we'll examine what happens when God disciplines us like a loving parent trying to impress upon a child to stop running into traffic or other dangerous actions. Perhaps you've had that experience of trying to impress upon a child the importance of staying safe. If the child doesn't listen, sometimes you need to use discipline to help the child to understand.

God's discipline to help us to stop repeating dangerous actions, is His way of caring and loving us by trying to get our attention. When God disciplines us, it wakes us up and gets our attention. It's hard-won lessons that aren't easily forgotten or ignored.

It's comforting to read Hebrews 12:6: "For the Lord disciplines the one He loves, and He chastens everyone He accepts as His son." Even though it says "son," this verse refers to all Christians, male and female. Once we're saved, we're adopted into His family as God's child (Romans 8:15; Ephesians 1:5).

The first time I really grasped this, it was like a weight lifted from my shoulders. God disciplines us because He loves us - not because

He's angry or trying to punish us. That love, though, sometimes means walking through uncomfortable and difficult situations to shape us into who He's calling us to be. Instead of rescuing us out of the consequences of our sins, God allows us to wallow in the consequences, so that we won't keep repeating the same mistakes.

I used to struggle with the idea of discipline. It felt harsh, like a correction I didn't want to face. But over time, I've realized that God's discipline is about molding us. When we're in a season of discipline, we're not necessarily fighting off the enemy's attacks. It's God's way of refining us, like the silversmith melting the precious metal so it can be molded, shaped, and impurities removed (c.f., Proverbs 25:4).

When we're in the middle of a hard season, it can be easy to fall into confusion and ask, "Is this an attack from the enemy, or is God disciplining me?" And honestly, sometimes it takes time to know for sure. But when we look at the bigger picture, we see God's fingerprints all over it. God's discipline is never meant to harm us; it's meant to shape us, to make us more like Him. And even if it's painful for a season, it always produces a harvest of righteousness and peace.

God's discipline means that we've done something for which we need to repent. Repentance is our apology to God for our sinful actions, and a commitment to turn away from that sin. It's wise to pray for God to give you the strength to resist any temptation to sin.

Hebrews 12:5-11 tells us to "not despise the chastening of the Lord, nor be discouraged when you are rebuked by Him; for whom the Lord loves He chastens," and in Revelation 3:19 Jesus says, "As many as I love, I rebuke and chasten. Therefore be zealous and repent."

Whether your struggles are from God's discipline or from spiritual warfare, it's always a good idea to put on the Armor of God (Ephesians 6:10-18) and it's essential to trust in the Lord, submit to Him, and resist the devil (Proverbs 3:5; James 4:7).

Hebrews 12:11 says, "No discipline seems pleasant at the time, but

CHAPTER 22: WHEN GOD DISCIPLINES US

painful. Later on, however, it produces a harvest of righteousness and peace for those who have been trained by it." That verse always gives me hope when I'm struggling. God's testing, God's pruning, and God's discipline are opportunities for us to grow and learn.

Remember as you endure these struggles, that God hasn't forgotten you, nor has He abandoned you. It's so easy to feel isolated when we're enduring hard times, yet God is always with us. His discipline is *not* condemnation; it's correction. God disciplines those whom He loves. And that correction is born from His love for us. God is our Father and He wants what's best for His children, even if the process of getting there is temporarily uncomfortable.

Let's remember to pray, study our Bibles daily, and reach out to mature believers for support during these trials. If you're going through a season of God's discipline, pray for Him to reveal to you the lesson He wants you to learn so that you won't repeat the mistakes again. You don't need to endure these painful experiences alone. Growth isn't easy, but it's worth it.

Reflection Questions:

1. Can you recall going through God's discipline? What did you learn as a result?
2. Did you have any destructive habits in the past that you've stopped, as a result of God's discipline in your life?
3. When you were enduring God's discipline, what were some of the fears that arose for you? Was it a relief to realize that God was lovingly parenting you with discipline to help you?
4. How has God's discipline differed from the times when you endured spiritual warfare?

Chapter 23: Understanding Demons' Limited Power

I was appalled and terrified when I first realized demons were real, and that they were attacking me because I was a Christian! The thought of evil beings in my home seemed like a horror movie. Yet, the Bible tells us that demonic spiritual warfare is real and to be expected as Christians. The devil and his legion of fallen angels (demons) don't play fair, and they're out to win. They don't seem to realize that Jesus has already defeated them, and that Satan lost.

In the Bible's book of Job, we get a glimpse into the heavenly court where Satan stands before God and requests permission to test the obedient man, Job. Satan can't do a thing without God's consent! God allowed Satan to test Job, but with clear limits: "Behold, all that he has is in your power; only do not lay a hand on his person" (Job 1:12). Even during Satan's attacks on Job's health, wealth, and family, God set boundaries. No matter what we face, the enemy can't do anything without God's approval. That doesn't mean it's easy or painless, but it does mean that God is ultimately in control, even when we're in the thick of a battle.

This truth has been such a comfort to me, especially when I've gone through hard times. Yes, we live in a broken world, and we'll experience struggles. Jesus Himself warned us, "In this world you will have trouble"

CHAPTER 23: UNDERSTANDING DEMONS' LIMITED POWER

(John 16:33). Knowing that our troubles aren't random, and that God allows them for a purpose, helps me to breathe a little easier. How about you? Our suffering is never outside of God's loving and sovereign will.

Perhaps you've read 2 Corinthians 4:4 which states that Satan is "the god of this world" (some translations say that he is "the god of this age"). How do we reconcile that statement in view of God's sovereignty? It is not a contradiction.

The Bible explains that God is sovereign, meaning that nothing happens without His knowledge or permission, including the existence of evil. So, 2 Corinthians 4:4 means that the devil is temporarily influencing the world's lies and spiritual blindness. The devil deceives people and promotes a worldview that opposes God. Yet, the devil is a defeated foe through Jesus' shed blood on the cross.

Because of Jesus' sacrifice on our behalf, Christians aren't under the devil's dominion. The moment we were saved, we were transferred from the kingdom of darkness into the Kingdom of God (Colossians 1:13). Satan may be "the god of this world" who is deceiving the unsaved, yet he has no authority over us. We temporarily live in a world influenced by the devil's lies, yet we stand firm in Christ's victory. The devil may have some influence, but his limited power is fading fast as we await Jesus' return.

So, what can demons do to us? Well, first, they try to mess with our minds. Demons aren't mind-readers, but they can guess what we're thinking because they've studied humanity for thousands of years. Demons also try to plant seeds of doubt or fear.

Demons will tempt you to watch an unbiblical movie, listen to blasphemous music, or read a worldly magazine, and this media contains demonic propaganda which influences your thoughts about God and about yourself. That's why the Bible exhorts us to "have no fellowship with darkness" (Ephesians 5:11). We need to be discerning about the media we consume and pray for God's strength to resist temptation.

In 2 Corinthians 10:5, we're told to "take every thought captive to obey Christ." If we're having troubling or sinful thoughts, we need to repent and pray for God to set our thoughts back upon the straight and narrow path. We need to read the Bible to renew our minds to align with God's will and turn away from demonic "entertainment."

Demons also like to stir up chaos and confusion. Maybe you've noticed how one bad thing leads to another, like it's one trial after another. If we succumb to the devil's temptations, our sinful appetite is never satisfied and continues to spiral into deeper darkness. 2 Timothy 3:13 describes the sad progression of sin: "But evil men and imposters will grow worse and worse, deceiving and being deceived." Sinful actions can never bring us peace or joy, which only come from Jesus.

Demons also try to bring division in relationships, plant seeds of bitterness or unforgiveness, or make us feel isolated. We find peace in remembering that the Holy Spirit is with Christians through all trials. In John 14:16, Jesus promises that the Holy Spirit will be our Helper, our Advocate, and our Comforter. No matter what the enemy throws at us, we're never alone. The Spirit of God empowers us to stand firm, to resist, and to find peace during turmoil. It's also one of the reasons why God gave us instructions in His Word about the Armor of God (Ephesians 6:10-18) for protection from the demons' attacks.

While demons can influence our circumstances (especially if we yield to sinful temptation), the demons can't do whatever they want. They're still on God's short leash, and God will ultimately use the demon's spiritual warfare for His glory and for our good (Romans 8:28). Even when we're enduring frightening painful trials, God has His hand on us, and He's setting the limits on demons.

I think sometimes we forget how much power God has over the enemy. We tend to give the devil too much credit. Yes, he's powerful and deceitful, but he's not all-powerful. After all, the devil and his demons are created beings who fell. They have no real power. God is the One who has the final say.

Sometimes, the enemy tries to attack our identity and wants us to forget who we are in Christ. He wants us to believe the lie that we're failures, that we're unworthy of God's love, or that God can't use us for His glory because of our sinful past. Or the devil manipulates us to seek our identity elsewhere, such as our career, income, or social status. But the only identity that matters is being a saved child of God. Any other identity is just a foolish attempt at defining ourselves. As Christian women, we are beloved daughters of the King, who are chosen and dearly loved (Ephesians 1:4-5). That never changes, no matter how much the enemy tries to shake us.

Still, we can't be naïve or drop our guard. 1 Peter 5:8 reminds us, "Be sober-minded, be alert. Your adversary the devil is prowling around like a roaring lion, looking for anyone he can devour." While demons can't harm us beyond what God allows, they still seek ways to lead us astray. They want to distract us, to make us feel disqualified, or to pull us away from God's purposes. The demons don't want us to share the Gospel. Still, we needn't fear the demons, since we have the Armor of God to protect us (Ephesians 6:10-18), and with prayer, Scripture, and the Holy Spirit, we stand firm.

Reflection Questions:

1. Do you think that the devil influences certain movies, music, or other media in attempts to manipulate people?
2. How can you resist the temptations the demons try to manipulate with?
3. Have you ever felt unqualified to share the Gospel? How did you overcome this feeling, so that you could share the Gospel?
4. How does it make you feel to remember that God is in control?

Chapter 24: Don't Let the Devil Steal Your Joy or Peace

Joy and peace are the second and third fruit of the Spirit listed in Galatians 5:22. The moment we believe the Gospel and Jesus becomes our Lord and Savior, the Holy Spirit indwells us. Joy and peace are amongst the evidence, or fruit, of salvation.

Yet, during struggles and trials, it can be difficult to feel joyful or peaceful. We know that James 1:2-3 tells us to "count it all joy" when we encounter trials that test our faith and produce endurance. Our heads may urge us to be joyful in trials, but our hearts may tell a different story.

I've found that since God saved me, I feel peaceful in ways that are illogical. When going through painful situations, I feel hopeful and trust that God will work things out for good. That wasn't always the case before my salvation, though, when I'd sometimes lose it when things didn't go as I'd planned. The peace of God is a ballast that keeps us level during stormy seas.

Yet, what about joy? Well, sometimes we confuse joy with happiness. Joy springs from the hope we have in Christ and the gratitude we have for God's grace in saving us. Joy is an eternal view, while happiness is contingent upon temporary externals such as whether things are going according to our plans. And that's the issue, isn't it, since our human plans are based upon our limited knowledge. Meanwhile, God is omnipotent and omniscient, so His plans are in charge.

Joy and peace aren't just fleeting feelings or things we have to "earn" in the middle of our pain. They're gifts that God offers us, even during our hardest seasons. So, it's possible to be unhappy in an earthly mortal sense, while still being joyful and peaceful inside because you have your eyes upon Jesus.

In fact, Jesus warned us in John 16:3, "In the world you have tribulation, but take courage; I have overcome the world." Tribulation, or hardship, is inevitable. But Jesus also gives us the key to how we can face these times: Take courage. It's not about pretending that things are fine when they're not. Remember how the Psalmist poured out his heart, including some "ugly" feelings, to God. Only the false religions insist that you "always stay positive, no matter what." Yet during our upsets and sorrows, we cling to the truth that Jesus has already overcome everything we face, and we can find peace in His victory.

God isn't caught off guard by our spiritual warfare and trials. He's not surprised by what we endure as Christians living on earth. Jesus endured it, too, and far worse than we ever will. Hebrews 4:15 says, "For we do not have a high priest who is unable to sympathize with our weaknesses, but one who in every respect has been tempted as we are, yet without sin." This means that Jesus understands your plight and your feelings. Turn to Him for strength and comfort.

We can't always control our circumstances, but we can control our response. Philippians 4:6-7 says, "Do not be anxious about anything, but in everything by prayer and supplication with thanksgiving let your requests be made known to God. And the peace of God, which surpasses all understanding, will guard your hearts and your minds in Christ Jesus." It's a reminder that prayer, gratitude, and surrender to God's will bring a peace that doesn't make sense in the natural world. It's supernatural, guarding our hearts and minds when we feel like we're sinking.

But choosing joy and peace isn't always as easy as praying a quick prayer or quoting a verse. Sometimes, the battle for peace feels like a long, exhausting journey. During those moments, we can also ask God to give us wisdom about any lessons that we need to learn from the trial. Psalm 119:71 says, "It is good for me that I was afflicted, that I may learn your statutes." Trials can be painful, yet they can encourage us to pray for the lesson we can learn from the situation. When we shift our perspective and look for what God is teaching us through the trial, it brings a sense of purpose and peace. We can see how the situation is helping us to grow.

Let us also be comforted by 2 Timothy 1:7, which says, "For God has not given us a spirit of fear, but of power and love and a sound mind." When fear tries to creep in, we can stand firm on the truth that God has given us the Spirit of power, love, and a sound mind.

As we discussed in an earlier chapter, the trial you're enduring may be part of God shepherding you in a better direction through pruning, testing, or disciplining. Ultimately, those situations - as painful as they are in the moment - are opportunities for growth.

During spiritual warfare or God's discipline, it's easy to fall into the trap of thinking that God is angry or punishing us. Yet, God disciplines those He loves (Hebrews 12:6), and His pruning process, though painful, is ultimately for our good. John 15:2 says, "Every branch in me that does not bear fruit He takes away; and every branch that bears fruit He prunes, that it may bear more fruit." If God is allowing a pruning season, it's because He's preparing us for greater fruitfulness.

During trials, the devil may encourage us to isolate and be alone. He may stir up division and arguments with our spouse or our friends. Beware of these traps! The devil may also tempt you to complain, which the Bible discourages: "Do all things without complaining and disputing, that you may become blameless and harmless, children of God without fault in the midst of a crooked and perverse generation, among whom you shine as lights in the world" (Philippians 2:14-15). 1 Corinthians 10:10 also says, "Nor complain, as some of them also complained, and were destroyed by the destroyer." In the story of the Exodus, we see consequences for those who complained.

Of course, God encourages us to take our complaints to Him and to be honest with Him about our fears. Yet, there's a difference between wallowing in complaining, and with admitting our feelings to God. Instead of complaining, we need to make our requests known to God (c.f., Philippians 4:6-7) and then trust His response to our prayers.

Again, resist the devil's attempts to isolate you. Ecclesiastes 4:9-10 says, "Two are better than one…For if they fall, one will lift up his companion." It's important to fellowship with other believers, and to confess our sins to one another. We also benefit by asking other believers to pray on our behalf. If you're shy about asking for prayers, pray for God to give you courage.

Joy and peace come from keeping our eyes on eternity. When the weight of the world feels too heavy, when everything around us seems to fall apart, remember that this is not our forever home. 2 Corinthians 4:17 says, "For our light and momentary troubles are achieving for us an eternal glory that far outweighs them all." The trials we face now are temporary, and they're producing something far greater than we know.

With God's help, we can shine the light of joy and peace so that others are blessed by our example. Our public display of trusting God in the storms, can encourage others to do the same. And perhaps you'll hear someone ask you what your "secret" is for being so joyful and peaceful during a trial . . . which is the perfect opening for you to share the good news of the Gospel with them!

Reflection Questions:

1. What are some helpful ways to deal with feelings of frustration?
2. How can you keep your eyes on Jesus during times of trials and struggles?
3. What are you grateful to God for? Have you praised Him recently for these blessings?
4. What are you looking forward to in Heaven?

Chapter 25: Unequally Yoked and Spiritual Warfare

If you're married to someone who isn't saved, or who's living in unrepentant sin, it can feel like spiritual warfare is all around you. Being unequally yoked can increase spiritual warfare, and here's why:

1. *A Divided House*

In Matthew 12:25, Jesus said, "Every kingdom divided against itself is laid waste, and no city or house divided against itself will stand." Marriage is a powerful union that reflects Christ's love for His Church, so when one partner is walking in darkness, it creates a divide.

This divide isn't just emotional or relational; it's spiritual. When you're a believer married to someone who isn't, there's a spiritual tension. You might feel pulled in different directions, spiritually isolated, jealous of equally yoked couples that you meet at church or even tempted to compromise your own faith to keep peace in the marriage.

The enemy wants to drive a wedge between you and your spouse, and he wants to sow seeds of doubt, frustration, or bitterness in your heart. You're battling not just for your own faith but for the soul of your spouse as well.

2. *The Enemy Targets Families*

Satan wants to destroy families, and marriage is the first line of defense in the family unit. Ephesians 5:31-32 emphasizes the importance of the marital relationship, and how it mirrors Christ and the Church. The devil knows that if he disrupts that union, he can weaken the strength of your entire family. God hates divorce (Malachi 2:16), but the devil celebrates divorce. When a spouse isn't walking with Christ, it can create an opening for the enemy to work, particularly in areas like emotional division, manipulation, or even fear.

The Bible calls the devil "the accuser" and he whispers accusations to believers such as, "Your prayers aren't enough." Or, "Your spouse will never change." The accuser tries to make you feel small and powerless. But remember, the battle belongs to the Lord, and He is faithful. Your spiritual life doesn't depend upon your spouse's actions.

3. *Strain in the Home*

Living with a spouse who is unrepentantly sinning can be maddening. The Bible warns us about how unresolved anger can give the devil a foothold in your life: "In your anger do not sin: Do not let the sun go down while you are still angry, and do not give the devil a foothold" (Ephesians 4:26-27).

It's normal to feel angry and frustrated when a loved one rejects the Gospel and continually defies God's commandments. But please give this anger to God, and don't go to sleep angry. The devil is always seeking entry points to cause havoc, and we don't want to give him extra avenues by going to sleep angry. Pour out your heart to God as you're falling asleep, instead of hanging onto anger by yourself.

4. *Isolation and Loneliness*

If your unsaved husband won't attend church with you, nor socialize with other Christians, then the temptation may be strong for you to stop attending church or fellowshipping. In a Christian marriage, the

CHAPTER 25: UNEQUALLY YOKED AND SPIRITUAL WARFARE

husband is the spiritual leader. So, how is a Christian wife to deal with a husband who doesn't cover or lead her with Biblical teachings?

The Bible exhorts us to attend church for fellowship, growth, and participating in the Lord's Supper (and also baptism if you haven't yet been baptized). Hebrews 10:25 says, "not forsaking the assembling of ourselves together, as is the manner of some, but exhorting one another, and so much the more as you see the Day approaching." Going to church is important, even if your husband won't accompany you.

I also encourage you to attend a biblically solid local women's Bible study at your church or another church in your area. Women's Bible studies that focus upon reading the Bible (and not studying a false teacher, as some women's Bible studies are prone to do) are a wonderful place to meet sisters in Christ. The women I've met at women's Bible studies are prayer warriors! There's usually a time during the gathering when the group leader asks for prayer requests. Don't hesitate to ask them to pray for your husband's salvation, and for your strength as you deal with the related issues in your marriage.

Avoid the temptation to isolate yourself, which could lead to loneliness and self-pity. Isolation could also increase the enemy's ability to coerce you into joining your unsaved husband's sinful activities. Proverbs 18:1 warns about the dangers of isolation: "A man who isolates himself seeks his own desire; He rages against all wise judgment."

The enemy may even try to blame you for your spouse's unrepentant sin. He might cruelly tell you that it's your fault that your husband gets drunk daily, or that he cheated on you. The truth is your role is to continue to live out your faith. You can't change your spouse's heart, but God can.

5. *Biblical Application for Your Marriage*

God's Word warns against Christians marrying an unsaved person. Perhaps you were both unsaved when married and then you were later saved.

Here are some encouragements and exhortations in the Bible to help you:

a. **Pray without ceasing**. Pray for God to soften your husband's heart. Pray for an evangelist whom your husband would respect, to share the Gospel with your husband. Pray for God to save your husband out of sin and deception. Pray for God to give you strength to endure the spiritual warfare in your marriage.

b. **Put on the Armor of God**. As we've emphasized in this book, don't go into battles unprepared. Ephesians 6:10-18 reminds us to put on the full Armor of God to stand against the enemy's schemes. Guard your heart with the belt of truth, the breastplate of righteousness, the gospel of peace shoes, the shield of faith, the helmet of salvation, and the sword of the Spirit (the Bible), and stand firm.

c. **Don't hide your faith**. You may be the only Christian that your husband meets. So, you have an opportunity to be an example of Christlike behavior and to share the Gospel with your spouse. 1 Peter 3:1-2 says that husbands can be won to the Lord as he observes his wife's chaste conduct.

d. **Seek Biblical counseling and support**. Reaching out to Biblically solid and spiritually mature Christians can help you to navigate your marriage while your husband continues to unrepentantly sin. Your support system could include a biblical counselor, a Christian marriage support group, your pastor, or your women's Bible study teacher.

e. **Forgiveness and grace**. We need to remember the grace and forgiveness that God extended to us when we were yet sinners. We were dead in sins when God raised us from our sinful life (Ephesians 2:1-3). Those who are unsaved are spiritually blind. As frustrating as it can be at times, pray for God to help you to extend grace to your unsaved husband. Forgive him as Christ has forgiven you (Ephesians 4:32).

f. **Pray for wisdom**. If your husband has brought sinful materials into your home, pray for God to give you wisdom about how to handle this situation. These materials could be invitations to spiritual warfare. Pray for God to help you to have an honest discussion with your husband about the need to keep sinful materials out of your home.

g. *Trust God with your marriage.* We plant the seed by sharing the Gospel. We don't save anyone, as only God can save souls. As you continue to pray for your husband's salvation, trust God. Turn to God continually in prayer for help with your marriage. I pray that your husband will be saved and that you'll both enjoy a Christ-centered marriage.

Reflection Questions:

1. Do you sense that there's spiritual warfare in your marriage? What forms is this taking, and what steps have you taken to deal with it?
2. How can you protect your heart from the enemy's attacks, particularly when dealing with unrepentant sin in your spouse?
3. Have you clearly shared the Gospel with your husband? After all, the Gospel is the power of God for salvation to everyone who believes (Romans 1:16).
4. Are you making sure to fellowship with other sisters in Christ at church and Bible study?

Chapter 26: Guilt, Shame, and Spiritual Warfare

We all likely have past sins that we're ashamed of. Even those saved in childhood are aware that they've rebelled against God and their parents. Sin is a big deal, and the Holy Spirit convicts us with godly sorrow when we realize the depth of our sin.

This isn't trying to make you feel guilty though, sister. Most likely, you already carry a burden of guilt (feeling bad about what you've done) and shame (feeling bad about who you are).

It's true that we were all wretched sinners before Jesus redeemed us through His shed blood on the cross. Yet, the moment that we believed the Gospel and placed our life and trust in Jesus Christ, our sins were forgiven.

We'll continue to sin until we go to Heaven (1 John 1:10). The indwelling Holy Spirit uses "godly sorrow" which is similar to feelings of guilt, to convict us of sins we commit. Before we were saved, we had "worldly sorrow" when we got caught committing a wrong (2 Corinthians 7:9-10). But after salvation, we grieve when the Holy Spirit convicts us of sin, and we realize that we've rebelled against our holy God Who saved us.

The guilt that the Holy Spirit convicts us with, always points us to repentance and growth. The guilt that the devil tries to produce through his accusations leads us to defeat and shame.

In Revelation 12:10 Satan is called the "accuser of our brothers and sisters," who accuses them before God day and night. The devil's accusations never stop. He doesn't pause, doesn't take a break. His goal is to wear us down, to make us doubt God's love, and to question if we're really forgiven.

These accusations touch on things that we've actually done wrong. Yet, even when Satan's accusations are based upon reality, the way he uses them is twisted. His goal is to paralyze us, to keep us in bondage, to make us feel like we're not worthy of God's love, or that our sin is too big for forgiveness.

In Zechariah 3:1-5, we see Joshua the high priest standing before the Lord wearing filthy clothes which represent the sin and guilt he carried. And there stands Satan, accusing Joshua to God. The accusations are true, and Joshua's sin and filth are real. Yet God's response is not to condemn Joshua but to clothe him in rich, clean garments. God says to Satan, "The Lord rebuke you!" (Zechariah 3:2). Even in the face of Satan's rightful accusations, God chooses grace. He doesn't stand with Satan in his judgment. Instead, He offers redemption. Joshua didn't have to defend himself, because God was his defender.

We don't need to defend ourselves either. When Satan's accusations swirl in your mind, you have a choice: *"Do I try to justify myself, to prove my worth through my actions, or do I rest in the truth that Christ's grace is sufficient?"* Ephesians 2:8-9 says, "For by grace you have been saved through faith; and that not of yourselves, it is the gift of God; not a result of works, so that no one may boast." God's grace alone is your defense, dear sister, not your track record. Jesus' perfect righteousness which He propitiated to you on the cross is your defender.

While Satan is busy accusing us and reminding us of our sinful past, Jesus intercedes on our behalf and stands as our advocate. Hebrews

4:14-16 says that Jesus is our great high priest who sympathizes with our weaknesses because He too was tested while on earth (of course, Jesus never sinned). Because of Jesus, we can boldly approach God the Father's throne of grace. We don't have to hide or cower in shame. Christ's advocacy is constant as He pleads on our behalf (Romans 8:34;Hebrews 7:25).

Sometimes, Satan's accusations whisper that our sinful past disqualifies us from God's love. This hurtful lie from the devil might make us hesitant to approach God with our requests. So, we must keep reading our Bible daily to remember that our access to God is through Jesus, and not through our own merits. When Jesus died on the cross, the temple curtain to the Holy of Holies tore which rendered believers direct access to God.

When Satan whispers lies of condemnation, you can rest in the truth that you're clothed in Jesus' perfect righteousness. God sees you through the lens of His Son's finished work on the cross. You don't need to defend yourself; you just need to rest in Him.

Satan also uses accusations to discourage us from sharing the gospel. He convinces us that we're not qualified, and that our past mistakes disqualify us from telling others about God's grace. The devil's lies can convince us that we wear a scarlet letter "A" on our chests, and that others reject us because of our sinful pasts. We compare our shame and guilt to other women and church who appear to be perfect and seem to have it all together. Yet, we're *all* sinners (Romans 3:23) in need of Jesus our Savior.

We don't share the gospel because we're perfect or sinless; we share it because Christ's perfection and sinlessness have been given to us on the cross. 2 Corinthians 5:21 says, "He made Him who knew no sin to be sin on our behalf, so that we might become the righteousness of God in Him."

When we allow the devil to win and we focus upon our failures and shortcomings, it's easy to want to shrink back. Yet God calls you and all believers to rise up in His grace, to be bold because of who He is, not who you are. Satan knows that if you share the Gospel that there's a chance that person will start following Jesus instead of him. The devil therefore will lie, sow seeds of doubt, and accuse you so that you'll hesitate and won't share the Gospel. How tragic when a sister in Christ listens to Satan's lies and doesn't present the Good News of Jesus' life, death, and resurrection to unsaved people.

Keep in mind that the Bible is filled with stories of God using sinful people for His glory. Everybody in the Bible sinned except for Jesus, because humanity has a sin nature. So, don't allow the devil's accusations to stop you from evangelizing and bearing fruit for His kingdom.

We were bought by Jesus on the cross. We're forgiven, transformed, and clothed in His perfect righteousness. So, we can confidently share the Gospel because of what Christ has done for us.

In the midst of Satan's accusations, remember: You were saved by grace alone. Romans 8:1 tells us that "there is now no condemnation for those who are in Christ Jesus." Instead of living in shame, we can walk in gratitude for God's grace. We can be thankful that God saved us out of the darkness of our hell-bound sinful lives.

You're forgiven. You're set free. And when the enemy whispers lies about your past, remember that your identity is wrapped up in Him, not in your past.

Reflection Questions:

1. When Jesus said on the cross "it is finished," that meant that He defeated sin and death. So why do you sometimes worry about

your past sins? Is there any positive point to reflecting about your past?
2. What are some key differences between the Holy Spirit's convictions of your sins, and the guilt and shame that come from the devil's accusations?
3. How do you overcome insecurities about sharing the Gospel?
4. What are some ways to stop negatively comparing yourself to other Christian women?

Chapter 27: Reducing Your Vulnerability to Spiritual Warfare

Spiritual warfare is inevitable for Christians. It's not whether you'll experience spiritual warfare, but how much and how often. So, let's look at ways to reduce our vulnerability to spiritual warfare:

Repenting.
We can open ourselves up to spiritual warfare by holding onto unconfessed sin. As you know from studying the Sermon on the Mount, our sinful thoughts are equivalent to sinful actions. Unforgiveness, lust, not trusting the Lord, and hateful thoughts, for example, are invitations for the enemy to come in and wreak havoc. In many cases, the devil was responsible for sowing seeds that led to these sinful thoughts and heart conditions.

You might think, "It's not that big of a deal." Yet, sin is never harmless. The Bible is clear: "For the wages of sin is death" (Romans 6:23). Unrepentant sin always brings consequences, not just in our relationship with God, but in our spiritual well-being. When we refuse to repent and turn away from sin, we give the enemy a foothold in our lives (Ephesians 4:27).If you're holding onto unrepentant sin right now, the first step is simple: Confess it to God. Ask for His forgiveness. Let Him cleanse you from all unrighteousness (1 John 1:9). Repentance isn't just about saying sorry; it's about turning away from what you know is wrong and walking in the direction of God's truth.

Sometimes, we aren't aware of our sin, so we can also pray for forgiveness for unaware sins as well. Psalm 19:12 says, "Who perceives his unintentional sins? Cleanse me from my hidden faults." While we may be unaware of every sin, it's important to pray for God's forgiveness for anything we may have missed. We can trust that God is faithful to forgive all our sins when we confess them (1 John 1:9).

Avoiding New Age and Occultic Practices.

Using New Age or occultic items or practices can make us vulnerable to spiritual warfare. Any practice condemned in the Bible is a sin. Besides, why would we want to do anything for which our Savior Jesus died?

Deuteronomy 18:10-12 warns against engaging in occult practices: "There shall not be found among you anyone…who practices divination or tells fortunes or interprets omens, or a sorcerer or a medium…for whoever does these things is an abomination to the Lord." This was the Bible passage that God used to save me, when I realized that my former new age practices made me an abomination to God. Ever since, I've been urging people to leave the new age and to destroy new age products.

If you have any tarot cards, angel cards, astrology books, or similar items, I encourage you to get rid of them. These are all tools of divination, which means trusting in demons or wishful thinking instead of trusting in the Lord.

Some professing Christians twist Scripture to try to justify using horoscopes, yet the Bible condemns astrology. And contrary to false teachings, the Magi weren't astrologers.

I've also heard women argue that their Christian freedom and liberty allows them to do whatever they want, in a belief called "antinomianism" or lawlessness. Christian freedom means we can live according to our conscience and the Holy Spirit's leadings for practices that aren't condemned in the Bible. Christian liberty also means that once we're saved, we're now able to choose not to sin. Prior to salvation, we rebelled against God and couldn't stop sinning.

Relationships.

Some friendships or partnerships pull us away from God's truth, where we allow toxic influences to shape our thoughts, actions, and attitudes.

1 Corinthians 15:33 tells us, "Do not be deceived: 'Bad company ruins good morals.'" Some people pull us down, whether they're gossiping, encouraging sin, watching blasphemous movies, or otherwise distracting us from the Lord. Jesus said that we're "in the world but not of the world" (John 17:14-16), so we have to beware of unhealthy relationships becoming spiritual pitfalls.

You may wrestle with leaving such relationships and missing the opportunity to be a witness for Christ. That's fine, if you're the strong one in the relationship who actually shares the Gospel and points them to Jesus. However, take time to pray and be honest with the Holy Spirit. Is this person pulling you down and distracting you from Jesus? Do you find yourself pretending to be cool and avoiding Gospel discussions, so they won't be offended? Or are you able to openly share your faith with this person?

If you need strength and boldness to share the Gospel, or to leave a relationship that makes you vulnerable to spiritual warfare, pray for God to help you.

Media Influences.

It might seem harmless to watch the latest movie or get lost in social media drama, but can I tell you something? The enemy can use our media consumption as part of spiritual warfare. The devil tries to use this media to make us anxious, instead of trusting in God's sovereignty.

Philippians 4:8 reminds us: "Finally, brothers and sisters, whatever is true, whatever is noble, whatever is right, whatever is pure, whatever is lovely, whatever is admirable—if anything is excellent or praiseworthy—think about such things."

If what you're watching, reading, or listening to promotes sinfulness, it's time for a change. Most likely, the Holy Spirit is already convicting you to get away from this type of media. Pray for His help in eliminating cravings for these forms of "entertainment," and to instead turn your hunger toward Jesus and Bible study.

Reflection Questions:

1. Have you spent time today repenting for known and unknown sins? How did that make you feel?
2. Are there any media habits that you need God's help to change? If so, please pray for His help right now.
3. Are there any New Age or occultic items or practices that you're holding onto? If so, please pray for God to give you the strength to remove these practices and items.
4. Are you currently in a relationship that is negatively impacting your walk with Christ? If so, please pray for God to give you wisdom, boldness and courage to share the Gospel with this person, invite them to church with you, and create boundaries within the relationship.

Chapter 28: Insomnia, Nightmares, Sleep Paralysis and Spiritual Warfare

Nighttime can feel like a spiritual warfare battleground, such as sleeplessness that keeps you tossing and turning, terrifying sleep paralysis, or nightmares that feel like you're being pursued by darkness.

When I was first saved, I experienced terrible insomnia because I was aware of demons trying to inflict spiritual warfare upon me and my household. I tried deliverance ministries, self-deliverance, and listened to videos and read books with prayers that were "guaranteed to rout out demons." Yet, these only gave me temporary relief followed by increased spiritual warfare. I was exhausted from sleeplessness, and anxious from the demonic activity in my home.

It's one thing to have a rough night here and there, but when this pattern drags on, it can feel like the enemy is attacking your rest, your peace, and even your sanity. The enemy knows how precious your rest is, and he'll do whatever he can to keep you exhausted and anxious, so that you're too tired or insecure to share the Gospel with the unsaved.

The demons of spiritual warfare try to keep you from resting. Insomnia occurs when you feel too anxious to let go and sleep. Nightmares occur when your dreams are filled with frightening and realistic scenarios. Sleep paralysis occurs when your body seems paralyzed and you can't scream for help.

Several professing Christian women have also told me horror stories about demons trying to molest them in their bed. Whether this is a real or imagined terror, the similar pattern of women who've revealed this scenario shows that it's a spiritual warfare aspect to be dealt with.

Ephesians 6:12 says, "For our struggle is not against flesh and blood, but against the rulers, against the powers, against the world forces of this darkness, against the spiritual forces of wickedness in the heavenly places." This verse speaks of the reality that what we experience in the physical world is often influenced by the unseen realm. Spiritual warfare can affect our waking and sleeping hours.

Praise God that He has the devil on a short leash and ultimately the demons can't do anything without God's permission. 1 John 4:4 reassures us, "Little children, you are from God and have overcome them, for he who is in you is greater than he who is in the world." The enemy may try to make you feel small and vulnerable, but you have the might of the Holy Spirit living within you which is a strength the enemy can't match.

Certainly, you can take steps to ensure you have a better night's sleep by avoiding reading or watching anything that could make you anxious, such as the news or a scary movie. As we'll explore in the next chapter, I've found that listening to audios of the Bible as I fall asleep really brings relief from nighttime spiritual warfare. After all, the Bible is the sword of the Spirit in the Armor of God. It's also important to pray for God's protection while you sleep.

If you do find yourself having insomnia, sleep paralysis or a nightmare, try to focus your thoughts upon Scripture during the experience, drawing strength from the Word of God. Psalm 34:7 declares, "The angel of the Lord encamps around those who fear Him, and rescues them." Fearing God means that you're in awe of the Creator, and that you deeply respect that He has the power to cast someone into either Heaven or hell.

Another powerful tool is the act of worship, even in the middle of a nightmare or sleep paralysis episode. You can praise God in your spirit, thinking of all of the reasons why you're sincerely grateful to God. You can exchange the "spirit of heaviness" for the "garment of praise" (Isaiah 61:3 KJV).

As you face these moments, remember that you're not fighting this battle alone. God is with you, and He reassures us in Isaiah 41:10, "Fear not, for I am with you; be not dismayed, for I am your God; I will strengthen you, I will help you, I will uphold you with my righteous right hand."

Romans 8:38-39 is also reassuring: "For I am convinced that neither death, nor life, nor angels, nor principalities, nor things present, nor things to come, nor powers, nor height, nor depth, nor any other created thing, will be able to separate us from the love of God, which is in Christ Jesus our Lord."

I also love Psalm 4:8 which says, "In peace I will both lie down and sleep; for you alone, O Lord, make me dwell in safety." That's a promise we can stand on. When you're facing nighttime spiritual warfare, remind yourself that you're safe in God's presence. Even if the enemy tries to stir up fear, the Lord is your refuge.

As Colossians 2:15 reminds us: Christ "disarmed the rulers and authorities and put them to open shame, by triumphing over them in him." Jesus defeated the enemy on the cross through His sacrifice on our behalf.

Reflection Questions:

1. Have you ever called out to Jesus in the middle of a nightmare? How did He come to your help?
2. Have you experienced spiritual warfare at bedtime? How did you deal with it?

3. Have you noticed that if you're tired or anxious, that you hesitate to evangelize or share the Gospel? How can this be overcome?
4. Which Bible verses comfort you, and help you to unwind so that you can get some rest?

Chapter 29: Stick to What the Bible Says

If you're exhausted from spiritual warfare, it can be tempting to turn to quick fix promises for relief. The devil knows that if he grinds you into vulnerability, that you'd likely try anything to make it stop. Instead of trusting and following the Bible's guidance to put on the Armor of God, submit to God, and resist the devil, you become prey to false teachers who promise to cast out your demons. Or your co-worker recommends a new age healing session to bring you "inner peace."

It can sound appealing to hear about a method to make the demons go away for good. There are ministries and books that promise immediate results. Maybe they tell you that if you pray their specific prayers, or if you'll book a session with them (including maintenance deliverance sessions), the spiritual warfare will stop.

One danger is that "quick fixes" can take your eyes off the Gospel and make you focus more upon the enemy than on Christ. When this happens, you may obsessively fear that everything's being controlled by demons. Quick fixes can lead you to trust in human systems or man-made formulas rather than depending upon the sovereign power of God. People become dependent upon the quick fixes, instead of turning to God in sincere prayer and trusting the Bible.

These deliverance ministries will angrily argue that "Jesus gave us authority to cast out demons." Yet, *authority* isn't the point. It's about *efficiency*. Why would we send a toddler (humans) into battle with demons, when King Jesus promises that He is with us always? Demons are terrified of Jesus, not of deliverance ministers (even when they add the "in Jesus' name" tagline).

Besides, who in their right mind thinks that it's a good idea to argue one-on-one with a demon? Why would a being who is pure evil and who hates us, listen to our commandments, even when we add "in Jesus' name"? We can play "Buffy the vampire slayer" or we can pray for Jesus to help us. I chose the latter. Again, it's not about *authority*, it's about *wisdom*.

The demons may theatrically pretend to leave in response to a deliverance minister's commands, but they'll soon return. That's why deliverance ministries make their clients go to "maintenance sessions." Even the ministries that offer to perform exorcisms for free often pressure their clients for donations or "love offerings." Deliverance ministry is a big lucrative business, and they don't like anyone criticizing their business model (like Paul upsetting the pagan Artemis silversmiths in Acts 19:23-27)!

Then there's the books which offer formulaic prayers for you to recite to "rout out demons." I fell for this scheme when I was first saved and desperate for relief from spiritual warfare. We must turn to God in prayer for protection and wisdom in spiritual warfare situations. Yet, using formula prayers is a gimmick that uses the Lord's name in vain. God can't be coerced or manipulated to answer prayers. He wants our heart and our heart-felt prayers, not scripted prayers that we say like commands to make a dog do tricks. Decreeing and declaring is not Biblical! That's man-centered false teaching that twists Scripture. Really, these books are insulting to God and to us!

Another quick fix is the market for "protective charms" such as the evil eye pendant, dream catchers, idol statues, and crystals that are supposed to block "negative energy." It's a crying shame that professing

CHAPTER 29: STICK TO WHAT THE BIBLE SAYS

Christians put their faith in these man-made items, instead of in God and His Word.

Nowhere in the Bible are we told to turn to objects for protection. Idolatry, in any form, is something God warns us about throughout the Bible. Relying on these items is inviting the presence of something other than the Holy Spirit into your life. These items don't belong in the life of a Christian because they don't line up with the truth of who God is and what He has already done for us through Jesus. We are to trust in the Lord, not in idols.

Reflection Questions:

1. Do you own any evil eye pendants, or other objects that people use for protection? If so, how might they be distracting you from putting your whole trust in God for protection?
2. Have you seen those books or seminars that offer to cast out demons? Was there any temptation to try them, and if so, how did you resist this temptation?
3. Have you ever relied on something other than God for protection, even unknowingly? How did that affect your spiritual life?
4. How can you begin to trust God more fully with your safety and peace, instead of turning to items or practices that might seem like quick fixes?

Chapter 30: Listening to the Audio Bible

After I fell into the deceptive trap of deliverance ministry and false teaching books with formula prayers to rout out demons, I turned to the Bible for help. I should have started there, as God's Word is sufficient and gives us everything we need for every situation including spiritual warfare.

From the Bible, I learned about the Armor of God, submitting to God, resisting the devil, and the importance of trusting in the Lord. Not surprisingly, all these approaches helped to reduce spiritual warfare and decreased my insomnia and anxiety about demons.

Since the day I was saved, I read the Bible daily. I start each morning with reading a chapter of the Bible. It's "Bible before breakfast" and "Word before world."

In the evening as we're drifting off to sleep, my husband and I play an audio of a Bible book. Sometimes I listen to the entire book before sleeping, and other times I fall asleep as the audio Bible is playing. It's so reassuring to listen to God's Word.

I've been listening to an audio Bible book nightly since 2017 when I was saved. This practice has helped me to sleep better, and also to hear Bible passages that I didn't notice while reading them. After all, the Bible is the sword of the Spirit in the Armor of God.

I highly recommend listening to an audio of the Bible being read line-by-line (not a dramatization) to everyone who tells me that they're experiencing spiritual warfare. I like the free ESV Bible app with David Cochran Heath's narration. We must be discerning on some of the other Bible apps and narrators, as there are some false teachers who try to sneak in to mislead people. I also appreciate that the free ESV app has a timer for the audio. If you prefer KJV or another Bible translation, there are plenty of free apps and YouTube videos where a narrator reads the Bible line-by-line.

My husband likes to listen to Genesis and Revelation audios, and I prefer the New Testament epistles. If I'm upset, the book of James is very comforting with its reminders to "count it all joy" during trials.

I'm also soothed by listening to audios of the Bible while driving, especially in heavy traffic or other stressful situations. You can listen to the Bible while flying on an airplane, or while walking, biking, hiking, or wherever you have an audio device.

Reading the Bible is incredible, but listening to it adds a layer of depth. When you hear Psalm 23 for example being read aloud, it feels different than when you read it silently. The words feel more alive, more personal. "The Lord is my shepherd; I shall not want…"

The audio Bible also helps you to memorize Scripture, especially if you listen repeatedly to the same Bible books. This helps you to tuck Scripture into your heart, so you can readily recall it during times of trials. Audio Bible saturates your mind with God's Word, which is part of renewing your mind and developing a solid Biblical worldview. False teachings sound like sour notes to a mind that is attuned to the Bible.

The repetitive nature of hearing Scripture, especially when you listen consistently, helps to plant God's Word in your heart and mind. It's like when you hear a song repeatedly: before you know it, you're singing along without even thinking about it. The same thing happens when you listen to the Bible. It sticks with you.

The more that you listen, the more the words and truths of Scripture will bubble up into your thoughts throughout the day. Suddenly, God's

Word is just there, ready to guide and comfort you in moments of need.

Of course, audio Bibles are a compliment to reading the Bible and not a substitute. Read the Bible in the morning and listen to the Bible at night.

It's hard to be anxious or fearful when you're surrounded by God's promises. When the enemy tries to bring discouragement or lies, hearing God's truth can shield your mind and heart.

Psalm 1 talks about the person who is blessed because they meditate on God's Word day and night. When you listen to Scripture, it gives you the opportunity to dwell on it. You can listen to the same verse or chapter multiple times, each time pulling out something new. As you listen, you reflect, and those reflections deepen your understanding of God's truth.

Sometimes, the enemy wants to distract us, to keep our minds busy with anything other than God's Word. But when you listen to the Bible, you're intentionally blocking out the noise of the world and filling your mind with God's peace and presence.

Reflection Questions:

1. Have you tried listening to the Bible before? If so, did you hear parts of the Bible that you didn't notice when reading?
2. What are some moments during your day when you could listen to Scripture? How could you incorporate Bible listening into your routine?
3. How do you think listening to the Bible could help you in moments of doubt or anxiety?
4. What are some of your favorite Bible books to listen to?

Afterword

I pray that this book has been helpful for you in your walk with Christ. Spiritual warfare is inevitable for Christians, yet it doesn't need to interfere with our evangelizing and service to the Lord. The devil tries to persuade us that our sinful past is beyond forgiveness, yet we know that the moment that we believed the Gospel and put our trust in Jesus Christ as our Lord and Savior, that we were forgiven. We were given salvation, the indwelling Holy Spirit, a new heart, and a new life in Christ. Halleluiah! Praise God!

Nobody except for Jesus is sinless, yet as Christians we are cloaked in Jesus' perfect righteousness. We're also commanded to go and make disciples (Matthew 28:19-20). That includes helping professing Christians to avoid deception (Ephesians 5:11). Remember to pray for God to give you strength and boldness in proclaiming the Gospel, which is the power of God for salvation to those who believe (Romans 1:16).

All glory to God,
Doreen

About the Author

Doreen Virtue holds a Master's Degree in Biblical and Theological Studies (56 units) with highest honors from Western Seminary. She also holds Master's and Bachelor's degrees in Counseling Psychology from Chapman University.

Prior to her salvation at age 59 in 2017, Doreen was a new age teacher. Doreen was born and raised in New Thought and she spent 33 years as a member of Christian Science, Unity and Religious Science churches before segueing to new age in the 1990's. She spent 26 years in the new age before God graciously and mercifully saved her.

Now, Doreen warns others about the deceptions of New Age and New Thought, and points them to Jesus and Bible study.

Some of Doreen's pre-salvation publications are still being sold as used copies and bootleg copies, and she asks that these items published in 2017 or earlier be discarded as New Age deception is part of the devil's spiritual warfare.

You can learn more about Doreen's work at:
DoreenVirtue.com
Facebook.com/DoreenVirtueForJesus
Instagram.com/DoreenVirtue
YouTube.com/@Doreen_Virtue